Shaping
Your Faith

Shaping
Your Faith

a guide to a personal theology

C. W. Christian

WORD BOOKS, *Publisher*
Waco, Texas

SHAPING YOUR FAITH:
A GUIDE TO A PERSONAL THEOLOGY

Library of Congress catalog card number: 72–84156
Printed in the United States of America.

To Mom and Dad
who gave me
the gift of freedom

Contents

Introduction

THIS BOOK IS NOT A BOOK OF THEOLOGY! At least, it is not theology in the usual sense, that is, a passing down from those select and blessed souls called theologians of the truths once delivered to the saints and to be believed and confessed by the faithful. The person who reads this book as a theology textbook will be disappointed, for he will find many of the familiar themes untreated and most of the classic questions with which theology books deal unanswered.

It is not my intention in the following pages to give you a theology, except in the very special sense of helping you to develop your *own* theology, your own understanding of the Christian faith, of how it relates you to God, to the church, and to the exciting and awesome reality we call "the modern world." Therefore, rather than being a book of theology, the present essay is an invitation to become a theologian. It is a book on theological method, intended as a step toward the development of a theology which will be thoroughly Christian, but uniquely and personally your own. We will not be primarily concerned with answering for the reader the classic questions of faith—What is God like? Who was Jesus? How does he redeem us? What is the church and the Kingdom of God?—but with suggesting how such questions can be understood and with providing resources by which the reader can seek his own answers.

One of my theological colleagues has dubbed this project "do-it-yourself" theology, and this is a good description of what I have in mind in inviting you to become a theologian. But one connotation of the expression "do-it-yourself" must be avoided. In our society this phrase often implies dilettantism and imperfection. One is likely to undertake a do-it-yourself project without the seriousness of a professional. It is a diversion, a leisure-time preoccupation, which can be taken up or laid aside as the spirit moves. Nothing really depends on it. Or a person may undertake it because he cannot afford the professional. Most of my own home projects are undertaken for economic reasons, and my limited skills are always evident in the finished job. No one has to tell me that a professional job would be better. So, "do-it-yourself" is often a stopgap, an undesirable substitute for the real thing.

But the development of a personal theology should not be understood in either of the above senses. While there is certainly a kind of intellectual stimulation in the struggle to develop one's own faith, it cannot be undertaken in a spirit of fun and games. Personal theology is serious business, and will likely be sustained only by the person who is serious about his faith, and who has become convinced that for him, at least, everything depends on it. In fact, the traditional lay habit of accepting the doctrinal utterances of the professional theologians and clergy without question and without any effort to appropriate them personally reveals a far more significant lack of earnestness. Furthermore, the developing of a personal theology is not a stopgap substitute for a professional theology, but is the inescapable responsibility of the Christian who takes his faith seriously in the modern world. Since the forging of a personal faith is a demanding and sometimes disturbing task, many people seek to escape by the adoption of some ready-made professional theology, but *this* then becomes the undesirable expedient, the substitute for the real thing.

Since the way into theology I am proposing to follow may represent a somewhat new approach or direction for my readers, some general observations and cautions are called for in order that they may enter into the study which follows with open eyes. Thus I offer the following words of counsel: First, don't expect conclusive answers to theological questions, except, perhaps, in certain very limited areas. This is not because the writer has no ready-made answers he would like to market to his unsuspecting audience, but because to provide them would divert us from our purpose and frustrate the attempt to help the reader think theologically for himself. Now, the attempt of a professional theologian like myself to keep his opinions to himself is not without a kind of agony, and will, I am sure, not be entirely successful. I will not be able to keep my own theology out of the pages that follow, but it will appear chiefly in three ways: (1) in relation to methods and tools of theology, where the nonprofessional is apt to have the least experience and require the most assistance, (2) as illustrative of possible answers to the questions of faith or of methods of arriving at such answers, and (3) as honest confession at certain points where my own theological prejudices need to be known by the reader, so that he might wisely evaluate the advice I am offering.

Second, be prepared to flex old and unused mental and spiritual muscles, and also to reexamine and reevaluate those doctrinal and theological concepts which have provided the basis for your own Christian life. If one is unwilling to subject his "received" understanding of faith to the insights of his personal experience, then he is not apt to achieve any significant degree of progress toward a personal theology. Therefore the serious Christian must be prepared to open questions long closed and unsettle conclusions and ideas long settled, even including the religious insights most central to his own life of faith. This process of reexamination cannot be avoided, and much of the content of this book will be directed at helping you carry it out. It would be unfair, however, not to remind the reader that such a reexamination carries with it certain risks, for the outcome cannot be anticipated in advance. This is why many prefer to cling to the security of an authoritative church or creed, rather than to risk being unsettled in their beliefs. But the risk of pursuing a personal theology is basically the risk of growth. Every parent watches his children pursue maturity with real anxiety, for he knows the hazards the child faces and the manifold tragedies and perversions to which he is vulnerable. But he also knows that the risk must be taken, for the tragedy of arrested development is far greater. It is my conviction that the Christian of our day must open himself to the challenge of maturing faith, with all of its hazards and heartaches, because the consequences of an obscurantist faith for the church and for the individual are more serious still. We cannot keep the questions closed any longer because life has opened them for us.

What then will we seek to do in the chapters that follow? Four things, primarily. First, we will try to understand the nature of theology and the role which it plays in the life of the church and in the life of the individual Christian. Second, we will ask about the sources from which the Christian can draw the raw materials for his theology and the norms or criteria by which he can evaluate his own theological thought and that of others. Third, we will seek to develop attitudes and ways of thinking which will make possible a wholesome openness to the theological ideas and outlooks of others within the Christian community. Finally, we will examine in broad outline the major areas which must find expression in any distinctly Christian theology.

Two final words need to be spoken. The first concerns style and vocabulary. It is not intended that this book be an "easy" book, because the task it is addressed to is neither an easy nor a simple one. I hope, however, that it will not be dense or unreadable. In order not to add unnecessary burdens on the reader, an attempt has been made to avoid technical theological terms wherever possible, and especially in the first part of the book. Most of the technical terms employed, if not explained in the text, are defined briefly in the glossary of theological terms at the back of the book.

The final word concerns the prime requisite for achieving the most from the study we are undertaking. This book is addressed to a Christian audience. This does not mean that it is not to be read by one of another faith, or of no faith at all, or that it will hold no interest for or have no value for such a person. It does mean that the author stands within the Christian community, is committed to its fundamental truth, and that the character and organization of the book will reflect this commitment. Thus this book will be most useful to one who shares this stance, and the basic tool which one should bring to the following study, apart from a healthy curiosity about life and faith in general, is an interest in and to some degree an involvement with the historical community which calls itself Christian.

Ready then? Let's do theology.

PART ONE

Come on in, the Water's Fine

CHAPTER ONE

Getting Your Feet Wet

THIS BOOK IS AN INVITATION to become a theologian. Now such an invitation is unlikely to cause a stampede of the laity to the banners of theology. This is especially true in my own tradition, which has inherited from its Anabaptist and free church forebears a suspicion of authority in general and of formal theology in particular; but it appears to be true in varying degrees in almost all Christian fellowships. Where the theologian is not viewed with suspicion as the intellectual underminer of faith he is at least looked upon by the practical layman and even by the pragmatic parish minister as a harmless purveyor of more or less unnecessary mystification. To many Christians, theology also seems to lack clarity and substance, to be less like solid ground on which one can stand and act than like an ever shifting swamp in which he may flounder and even drown.

Fortunately for theology, however, and for the serious Christian, these impressions, while not entirely mistaken, are partial and inadequate. In my own case, the discovery of the value and function of theology in the Christian life was very much like my experience of learning to swim when I was a boy. I was able to quickly master the necessary form while stretched on the sunny apron beside the pool, but when I was forced to try it in the water I quickly lost my coordination and thrashed helplessly. My fear of the water paralyzed me. It became my enemy, my burden. It threatened to destroy me, to suck me under to my death. But then from an older friend I made a discovery: one learns to swim not by fighting the water but by using it. It could engulf me if I used it badly, but it could also support me if I learned to use it well. Indeed, swimming became pleasure for me when I could look upon the insubstantial and shifting fluid about me as the very stuff which enabled me to stay afloat, as something meant to buoy me up and not to drag me down.

The first step, similarly, in coming to understand why the church has so stubbornly insisted on having theologians and theology and in appreciating their value in your personal Christian existence is to recognize that their function, when properly performed and when properly accepted, is to buoy up the church and the Christian, to undergird his faith and to provide a solid support for the believer in the crises of mind and heart which challenge him almost daily in life. In fact, a primary reason for developing a personal theology is to transform theology from a liability to an asset in your own Christian existence. And so the invitation is to learn to swim, so to speak, in one's own baptismal waters and to begin to venture into the deeper waters of Christian experience with a new degree of self-confidence and understanding.

THE ROAD TO THEOLOGY

How does one make a beginning at being a theologian? In a certain absolute sense, he begins by being born, for the mere asking of the questions of meaning or value is the beginning of the theological quest; and these are as inescapable as life itself. In a narrower sense, he begins, as we shall see presently, by entering into the Christian experience of redemption. Although one may entertain the subjects of theology without a Christian commitment, his theology never becomes fully Christian except as it reflects a sense of forgiveness in Christ. Theology is born out of the crucible of sin, doubt and redemption. Every great theologian has shaped his theology out of the stuff of personal struggle. Paul's doctrine of the freedom of grace was born out of his agony of the law and his own deliverance through Christ. Augustine forged a theology which became the foundation of almost all Christian doctrine in the West, and he did so out of his own search for meaning and life in the midst of a dying culture. Luther knew whereof he spoke when he said that one becomes a theologian not by study but by living and dying and being damned.

Now the example of such giants as these might have an inhibiting effect on most of us. Must we have the kind of depth and intensity of experience that these men had in order to develop a personal theology? Not at all. There are reasons —sociological, psychological and historical—why their experiences and their resulting theologies loom so large in the history of the church. Most of us cannot hope to have the impact that these men have had. But one thing we have in common with them: our theology, if it is ours and if it is to contribute in a more limited way to the church and its self-understanding, must be existential. It must have at its core the redemptive experience in Christ. Theology remains academic and abstract unless it is given its impetus by the impact of religious experience.

However, if the question, "How does one become a theologian?" is one of theological method—that is, of what questions one first seeks to answer and how and where he finds answers—then the possible points of departure are almost unlimited. There is no single proper starting point, as will be explained below. Wherever we choose to begin, it is well to keep in mind that we are asking at the moment about *theology* as a human activity and as an activity of the church, not about

God. Thus our first need is to observe the church as it does theology, and ask what it is that we do when we speak of God.

Why Do We Fear Theology?

I have already suggested that most Christians, both lay and clerical, are fearful or suspicious of theology and I have suggested in a general way why this is so. We need to look more carefully at this negative mind set in order that we might discern the various strands which make up the fabric of suspicion, and in order that we might more objectively evaluate each. There are, accordingly, a number of causes for what, in the final analysis, I hope to show to be an unjust fear:

1. *Its practitioners.* One reason for suspicion of theology is to be found in attitudes cultivated by theologians themselves. For many centuries and in most communions those whose job it has been to study and formulate the church's doctrine have often encouraged theological ignorance among the laity and even to some degree among the lesser clergy. For the most part it must be confessed that the motives behind their efforts to cultivate a nontheological laity were not admirable. By keeping the people theologically naïve they were able to perpetuate a religious caste system and to secure a peculiar prestige and influence within it. Furthermore, both political and religious control could be exercised on a people who in their ignorance were forced to depend on the theologian for right guidance in the very saving of their souls. While the Reformation and the more recent triumph of the free church tradition in most of Western Christendom has lessened the power of the theological class, there is still a certain temptation for the theologians to form a professional caste and to be somewhat jealous of their prerogatives. More significant, there still persists in many lay Christians a kind of hesitancy to become involved in Christian thought and a sense of unworthiness and inadequacy for theology.

Such a theological inferiority complex, which is almost certainly a relic of the past, can no longer be justified. In other centuries it was often true that the vast majority of Christians did not possess even the rudiments of the education required to master Augustine or Thomas Aquinas, or to rightly divide the Council of Chalcedon. Thus in some degree the reservation of theology to the universities and the specialists was justified. One couldn't trust the interpretation of Scripture, for example, to a peasant who couldn't even read the Pater Noster. But this situation no longer exists. Most Christians today possess entirely adequate intellectual tools for a fruitful and creative participation in the shaping of the church's faith.

Those of us who do theology as our vocations have been slow to recognize this fact, but John A. T. Robinson is surely correct that the time has come for the professional theologians and church leaders to learn to trust the laity. More so, we must encourage the laity to trust themselves. The theologians must run the risk of speaking freely to the people and the people must run the risk of hearing with open ears and of becoming involved in the theological process.

2. Its complexity and obscurity. Now, the "theolog" must confess that theology is often unnecessarily complex and obscure. There is a kind of intellectual pride which takes delight in creating an impression of unutterable profundity for its own sake. It becomes the status symbol of the caste and is a modern expression of the Gnostic tendency in the early church to create an intellectual elite, a church-within-the-church, an inner circle of true disciples who possess the secret of wisdom and truth. The Christian need not be put off from theology, however, by this pseudocomplexity, because it does not represent theology as such.

On the other hand, there is a certain complexity in theology which is inescapable at certain levels of theological inquiry. There is, to begin with, a complexity which results from the continuing refinement of theological language for the sake of accuracy and precision. Theologians find that they must develop a technical vocabulary in order to express subtle shades of meaning which common language often will not express. In this the professional theologian is no different from the professional or technician in any other specialized field of study. Just as a specific medical terminology evolves in order that specialists in medicine can communicate with each other, so also theologians have tended to develop a specific theological vocabulary and language. However, it is not necessary for the church member to master this technical vocabulary in order to come to a sound basic understanding of faith, any more than it is necessary for one to become a medical specialist to have a sound grasp of mental and physical health.

But there is a second reason why theology must be complex. By its very nature, it is concerned with God as the source and meaning of life. Thus theology seeks to see *wholly*, to understand all of life in the light of God's creative and redemptive purpose, and life is not simple. Thus in principle theology is committed to total understanding. In practice, however, no theologian can approach this total vision, and again the essentials are capable of being grasped with a degree of genuine clarity by any Christian of broad sympathies and serious intentions. This means that despite the apparent and even real complexity of theology we cannot allow ourselves to be deterred from seeking a personal understanding of faith.

3. *Its seeming irrelevance to life.* The irony of traditional theology lies in the fact that while it aims at understanding all of life, it so often seems, even to the interested Christian, to occupy itself with matters peripheral to the main concerns of living. While as men we are concerned with decision-making, with concrete ethical problems, with questions of family, vocation, and politics, theology is concerned with the two-natures doctrine, total depravity, and the Trinity. A few years ago an intelligent Christian lawyer confided in me that while he tried to be an orthodox believer, for the life of him he could not see how it made him a better Christian or a better man to believe that three is one and one is three. And isn't this

attitude common among lay Christians? Indeed, the classic
image of the theologian for many is the medieval scholar, di-
vorced from life by the walls of a monastery or isolated from
the world in the halls of academe, debating with his learned
colleagues on how many angels can stand on the head of a
pin. And a theologian like myself cannot expect to see any
real interest of the church member in theology unless this
sense of irrelevancy is overcome.

What shall I say to this matter? I must first admit that theologians (more so, I think, than theology) do often become de-
tached from life. This is the temptation of theorists and
specialists in every field. Now, make no mistake, theory is
always born out of practical experience. Behind Einstein's general theory of relativity lies the hardheaded experience of
practical men—like Galileo, Newton, Kepler, Michelson and
Morley—with time, light, stars and stones; and behind the
two-natures doctrine lies the church's very real experience of
redemption through Christ. Theory grows out of the concreteness of experience and the questions it raises. Pure research is
never, in the end, abstract. But the experts' concentration on
the theory of a science or of an art may cause them to lose the
feeling for life as it is lived, and with the points at which their
theory makes contact with practical experience. And the gap
between theory and practice may grow progressively wider
for each generation. We may fail to replace language and
concepts which no longer carry meaning. We may neglect to
wrestle with new problems thrust upon us by the changing
world, preferring the comfort of familiar sounding and time-
hallowed formulas.

The danger that theology may become irrelevant is always
very real. But this very danger is again a potent argument for
lay theology. While trained theologians are necessary to do the
technical labors, informed lay theologians, who are far more
deeply immersed in the currents of daily life, are essential to
keep the theological community relevant. A major reason
why medieval theology bogged down in irrelevancy was that

it lacked such an informed laity. Without it, the professional theologian always ends up answering questions which no one is asking.

The blame for the kind of irrelevance described above is chiefly the theologian's, but the layman is not without guilt in the matter. Theology may appear irrelevant because the layman has not made the effort to understand, to learn how to distinguish between the language in which traditional theology speaks and the meaning which it seeks to convey. One of the goals of our study will be the developing of theological sensitivity, that is, the cultivation of the skill of perceiving what people are seeking to express by the sometimes imprecise language of doctrine. Much of the language of faith may be empty of meaning for us and therefore may rightly be abandoned, as my own fellowship, for example, has largely chosen to abandon certain doctrines of the medieval church. However, the honest examination necessary to determine whether or not particular doctrines are indeed empty and without value may lead us to discover that much traditional theology, while it speaks in the language of past centuries, addresses itself to questions and needs of life which are profoundly contemporary and relevant. One of the great thrills of developing a personal theology is the rediscovery of the great voices of our faith from the past, and the sudden recognition that they are indeed our kinsmen—that though they wore beards and dressed in togas or in the robes and hoods of monks, they knew the same needs, asked the same questions, and found the same hopes and securities as we.

The final reason for the seeming irrelevance of theology touches the heart of our purpose in this study, for it concerns the very problem we are seeking to overcome. Theology often seems irrelevant to the Christian precisely because it is not his own. It is inherited theology; it has been handed down to him with the approval of the proper authorities, with the high recommendation of the church, and frequently with the warning that he must believe it under penalty to his soul. But though we may try earnestly to believe, an inherited theology is not our own theology, and can never quite fit the particular needs and peculiar ways of thinking, living, deciding which are distinctly our own. A theology which is somebody else's theology, even if it be Augustine's or Luther's or even Paul's, is necessarily to some degree irrelevant. A second- or third-hand theology is no more adequate than a second- or third-hand experience of grace. As a second son, I learned at an early age that hand-me-downs were never quite my own. Though I wore them, I was constantly reminded by the shallowness of their cut here and the unneeded fullness there that they had been tailored for somebody else. So the Christian has no right to dismiss the traditional doctrinal expressions of the church's faith or the seemingly exotic concerns of other Christians as irrelevant until he has won his way through to an expression of *his* faith—a *theology*, mind you—which, while deeply indebted to his Christian past, yet bears the mark of originality and of his own person.

4. *An anti-intellectual attitude.* The fourth reason for our hesitancy toward theology can be disposed of quickly. I refer to the anti-intellectualism which is traditional within many Christian communities. Such an attitude is especially common within those denominations which are descended from the "peoples-churches" of the Reformation period, the Anabaptist and spiritualist groups. But other churches which have grown up on the frontier in America and have drunk deeply of the Populist tradition have a similar disdain for the religious egghead. Now the value of this traditional attitude lies in the fact that superior intellectual achievement and superior theology are no guarantee of the possession of the Spirit of God. A sound theology does not make a religious man. And a man may allow his intellectual pride to be a substitute for a humble walk with God. However, we in the nontheological traditions have often drawn a dangerous conclusion from this truth. We have believed that if too much learning is a dangerous thing, then no learning at all is better. We have con-

cluded that theological simplicity or ignorance *does* guarantee the Spirit. This is not the case. There is an arrogance of the ignorant which is no more savory or Christian than the arrogance of the erudite.

Indeed, one advantage of serious thought about one's faith is that it may lead him to see the limitations and the human fallibility of his own opinions, and therefore open him up to others with a certain humility and graciousness, while theological ignorance may cause one to identify his prejudices and opinions with the prejudices and opinions of God.

An illustration from another area may help. In my experience, the more catholic and sophisticated the musical taste and experience of a person, the more apt he is to see the value of the simpler and less sophisticated forms enjoyed by the untrained. Thus a Leonard Bernstein can highly regard jazz, rock, and country music for its very real values. But how many admirers of country music will concede the value and meaningfulness of Bach or Haydn? Similarly, theological simplicity often leads to a kind of pietistic snobbism in the church, and this is most unbecoming. Several years ago a well-meaning religious editor discussed a biblical question in his periodical. He listed and rejected several possible understandings of the passage under consideration on the grounds that they were "interpretations"; then he gave "the true meaning" of the passage, apparently oblivious to the possibility that this was *his* interpretation. Such a confusion of our own views with God and the dismissal of every other view is not the result, usually, of bad will but of poor understanding. It calls for a better personal theology.

5. *Inertia.* The final, and perhaps the most potent reason for our hesitancy to become theologians lies in the inertia which flesh is heir to. And our initial laziness is complicated by the pressures which are a part of contemporary society. The incredible enlargement of knowledge and complexification of life in the twentieth century have done away with the universal genius.

No man in our time can know all there is to know or be all things. Thus our day has become the day of the expert, and we have become accustomed to trusting increasingly large areas of our lives to the governance of the specialist. This acceptance of "the authority of the authority" has reinforced the natural tendency of the laity in the church to accept the work of the theological and clerical specialist and to leave it at that. To this tendency toward "specialism" it must be urged that not all areas of life are equally subject to the authority of expertise. Technology requires it, but in those areas which must finally determine the uses, limits, and values of technological and sociological processes—those which ask the questions of human values, such as ethics, philosophy, and religion—we cannot surrender the attempt to see life as a whole to the fragmentary viewpoint of the specialist, nor can we surrender the personal responsibility to see life *for ourselves*. Thus the church must call its people back to the task of doing theology.

Some Basic Matters

Until now we have been assuming a common agreement on the nature and character of theology. We must now establish a clearer and more historically correct understanding of our subject. We need a working definition of theology and of the other terms more or less commonly associated with it. The reader should keep in mind, however, that definitions are descriptive, not determinative. By this I mean that the dictionary does not determine the meaning of a word; it merely describes the way it is used by people. This is why an unabridged dictionary will often list a large number of alternative and even unrelated meanings for a given word. These are the actual historical ways it has been and is being used. The definition or description of theology I will offer below is this kind of definition. I am not attempting to set forth a theory of what theology is or should be, but I am trying to describe theology as it has actually been understood and, more important, as it has really been done by the church. My primary intention is to help the reader to judge from his own experience whether this description is accurate.

1. *What is theology?* The word *theology* is derived from the Greek *theos*, meaning "god," and *logos*, which means literally "word"; but in compound forms logos carries the broader meaning of discourse, knowledge, wisdom or thought about the subject under discussion. Theology therefore means in its most proper sense "thought or discourse about God." Strictly speaking, then, theology is our thought about God as distinct from our understanding of man, Christ, sin, etc. Since, however, God as creator and redeemer is involved with all of life, the term has come to apply to all thought which has to do with man and creation as they relate to God, or, more briefly, to all serious religious thought.

A related term is *doctrine* from the Latin *doctrina*, "teaching." While the terms theology and doctrine are sometimes used interchangeably, doctrine refers more properly to those theological teachings which have achieved a more or less official acceptance by a particular denomination or by the church at large. Thus we may speak of Lutheran doctrine or Christian doctrine. Generally speaking, then, theology is the more comprehensive term, and there has been much theology—thought about God—outside of what could properly be called doctrine.

A third word, *dogma*, from the Greek meaning "to seem" or "to seem good," is a word with an evil connotation for most Americans, since it has come to mean teachings which are arbitrary, authoritarian and—well, "dogmatic!" Technically speaking, however, dogma means those fundamental truths of doctrine officially proclaimed and maintained by a church. It is therefore a still more exact term than theology or doctrine. In the discipline of theology, the term dogmatics is often used to mean the systematic exposition of the theology of the church, or what is more commonly referred to in Amer-

ica as systematic theology. Thus Karl Barth has written in
Germany his great *Church Dogmatics,* while Paul Tillich, who
wrote his work of the same sort in America, called it *Systematic Theology.*

2. *Where do we get theology?* Theology comes from experience. Now, this statement should be carefully considered by
the reader, for it represents a kind of watershed in our present
study. The person who is unable to follow me at this point
will probably not wish to pursue the study any further. His
unwillingness will probably mean a mind set against recognizing any human element in the theology or doctrine of the
Christian faith, and the recognition of the human dimension
of doctrine is demanded by the clear history of the church and
by our own Christian experience, rightly understood. But in
order that you might follow me with better conscience, let me
explain the sense in which the statement is true and significant for our purposes.

Theology derives from experience. So far, so good! This
judgment should create no problems. So does everything else
derive from experience! Our views on economics, on politics,
our ethical ideals, our opinions on social issues, our loyalties
—all are the products in some degree of our total life experience. An infant has no economics, no politics, no ethical ideals,
and only a single, essentially biological loyalty to himself.
This is because he has virtually no experience, especially no
social experience, out of which his selfhood and the increasingly complex network of ideas which we call mature personality can grow. For the same reason, he has no theology. And
just as his understanding of the other areas of life comes
jointly from the world about him and from his reaction to and
participation in that world, his theology emerges from his reaction to life as he experiences it.

But isn't theology from God? Has not the church always
maintained that its theology is more than a commentary on
life, and that it speaks with a divine authority? True, but it
must be pointed out that no matter how strong one's doctrine

of revelation or how profound one's experience of the reality and presence of God, this revelation must take place and must be appropriated in and through his personal experience. If one speaks, another must hear—if there is to truly be any communication. And not only must we encounter God within our general experience, we must also bring our minds to bear on this reality, this experience, this word, and come to an understanding of what it means *to us!* This is precisely the process which we each go through at every stage of our religious development. We undergo an experience with God, we share in the communal life of the church, we listen to the words spoken to us in worship and instruction, and then, whether consciously or otherwise, we draw them together, relate them in thought to other areas of our experience, and create an understanding of God and religion which is uniquely our own.

Notice what this means. It means that while the elements of our budding theology—for this is what it is—have come to us from without (from God, from the church, from life), it is in the final analysis, *our* creation, our mental construction. The whole which unites experience and constitutes our theology is the product of our mental effort. It is our reaction to life and to God. Just as one's physics is his own understanding of the physical world derived from his physical experience of that world, so also is our theology our understanding of God, man, and creation in the light of our religious experience; or, if you prefer, it is our response to God as he confronts us in nature, in the church, in Scripture and in our hearts.

If the above observations have been grasped, we are ready now to formulate the working definition which will guide us through the remainder of this study. *Theology is the verbal expression* (whether spoken or thought) *of religious experience.* Theology is *our thought about* God and about all the experiences we have which have anything to say about God. It is the attempt of the believer to give expression—as consist-

ent and accurate as possible—to the experience which to him
often seems to lie too deep for words.

Now this definition is as true of the church's theology as it
is of the individual's. The theology of the church is the attempt of that fellowship to find words adequate to describe
the divine reality which it experiences in its midst, that is, to
speak of its common possession and presence. And the
church's thought about its experience of God is the collation
of the thought of its people in worship and service. Indeed,
the religious experience of the individual as well as his theological understanding of it become a part of that century-
long struggle of the church to understand its faith which we
call the history of Christian doctrine.

3. *Some surprising(?) conclusions.* We are ready now to
draw some conclusions which will prepare us for some important questions to come. The peculiar way in which this
paragraph has been headed reflects the writer's hope that the
meaning of the preceding paragraphs has been taken seriously,
for then the conclusions we are about to draw, and which
might fall with a most uncertain sound on unprepared ears,
will seem both reasonable and orthodox. They will follow, to
quote a nontheological pedant, "as the night the day."

First, theology is not unchanging! Now, if one identifies
theology with God and understands theological doctrines to
be eternal truths handed down by a golden cord from God for
all ages, then the suggestion that theology may change is unacceptable. But it is very difficult, it seems to me, to consistently maintain a doctrine of unchanging truths for the simple
reason that human language changes and that theology is inescapably bound to language. The fact that theologians now
speak in German and English rather than in Greek and Latin
imposes the fact of change upon our theology. And with every
enlargement of our language by new experience, the richness of its capacity for thinking about God is enhanced. Thus
if theology is our attempt to unite all of our experience with
our understanding of God, then potentially our theology

can change with each new experience in the world. Theology changes continually.

A moment's thought will reveal the degree to which our personal theology is in a constant state of flux. Every minister knows the experience of looking back over the sermons he preached in seminary days and being embarrassed to think that he inflicted such trash on his people. His shock is partly from realizing the immaturity of his rhetoric and the weakness of his organization, but he is also shocked at the inadequacy of his thought content. He is apt to say to himself, "I can't preach this sermon again; I don't believe it anymore." As a teacher I have been amazed at the amount of "bad" or poorly thought-out theology I dished out in my early years of teaching, as witnessed by my old lecture notes. And what Christian will not admit that in previous years, or perhaps as a child, he strongly held beliefs about God to which he could not now give unqualified assent. In every case we are confessing that in some measure our theology has changed as life has changed.

More positively put, we can say that theology is dynamic. It is, like life itself, in a constant state of growth. And if theology is our understanding of life in the light of God, then how could we have ever expected it to remain static when life itself is a process of continuing enrichment? A theology frozen at an adolescent level is inadequate for a mature person. On the other hand, the maturing Christian should be able to say things about faith now which were not formerly possible. And once again what is true of the individual is also true of the church. The church's doctrine must also be rethought, clarified and deepened as it moves through the centuries, so that the theology of the modern church must surpass in richness and in comprehension that of the Reformation or of the classical period and, in significant respects, even that of the Apostolic church. This is because it has new centuries of life and history to digest and deal with. It cannot choose not to deal with new facts of life without suffering for it. The agony which the church has undergone in the last century by not coming to terms with, for example, Darwin and evolution, proves that an unconfronted experience lies just as heavily upon the religious stomach as does an undigested midnight snack in the hours before dawn.

Now the idea that theology is changeable, even when it can be supported by logic and evidence, may nevertheless be deeply troubling to the reader, since it seems to take the ground out from under our feet. There are few enough things that are secure. Yet we have been taught to believe that some things are certain in life and we have rested our spirits on these certainties. What is to happen if we now accept the conclusion that these also change? What remains as firm and sure?

Now, we must not and cannot deny the necessity for a certain foundation for life if it is to be whole and creative, and it is all too easy to attack the supports on which the lives of people rest. But it is important that the foundations we build on be sound and true, or they may fail us in crisis. To rest our faith and hope on belief in unchanging doctrines is a risky business at best, for when these doctrines prove untenable everything is placed in jeopardy. But where then can we find a true foundation if theology changes? The answer must be that God alone is firm and sure, not our thought about him. We must recognize again the distinction between the God who is the final source and end of our theology and the always inadequate and shifting way in which we comprehend him. God as he is for us does not change, but our experience of him and our thought about him change.

The dependence of the believer on infallible doctrines, or the identification of these truths with God, can be religiously dangerous. The time is apt to come when the old doctrinal language no longer seems adequate to his experience, and in concluding that his theology is not true he may conclude that God is also unreal. He will be unable to see that it is his theology which is at fault and not God. Many a college student has identified God with his boyish understanding of him and concluded he could no longer believe. In some degree the recent theology of the Death of God represents just such a repudiation of all theism in the name of rejecting an inadequate view of God inherited from the Middle Ages without modification. By recognizing the changeable human character of theology we are free to constantly examine and revise it in the light of faith and of God. "Let God be true, and every man a liar."

Second, theology is not infallible. Now in saying this we are being even more explicit and bold than we were in the preceding paragraphs. Theology not only can change, it can also err. What has been said above might be understood to mean that our earlier understandings were inadequate simply because they were incomplete. Not wrong, just not fully developed or explicit! This is often the case, but theology can also be wrong. This is again because theology is not God, but a human activity, a thinking about God which never measures up to the fullness of God and is never immune to error. Since theology is human it is subject to all the foibles that flesh is heir to. It can be misled, distracted or even perverted by secret sins of the theologians. It can be misshapen by the prejudice of groups or congregations. Nor can we be sure that our progress is always away from error toward greater truth. Which one of us who knows he has mistaken truth and misunderstood God in the past can believe that he will not make other, perhaps greater errors in the future? Theology is human; therefore it is not infallible.

Finally, a man's (or a church's) theology is not his faith. It is obvious that his faith and his theology are related, but they are not identical. Theology is a secondary activity, one step removed from his real religious life. This is why a person can have an ever so proper theology and have little depth or genuineness in his religious life; and this is also why he can have a very real relation to God and yet, because of inadequacies in training or background, can express his faith in a very faulty theology. Furthermore, the recognition of this fact makes possible a new kind of understanding among Christians, since it is no longer necessary to assume that disagreements on theology mean differences in faith. A new kind of charity is possible toward one another and toward Christians in other confessions when we understand that theological error does not necessarily mean unfaith. Such a recognition also helps us to understand how the lives of individual Christians and of churches whose theology is so far from the mainstream as to border on heresy can still produce the "fruits of the Spirit." Their real religious life is lived at a deeper and truer level than their theology, which is a human fallible creation of their faith.

SUGGESTIONS FOR THOUGHT
AND DISCUSSION

The following thought and discussion suggestions are intended to provide the individual reader or group with a beginning at "doing theology." I have avoided "feedback" questions and sought to stimulate the reader to begin the adventure of a thinking faith.

1. Analyze your own attitudes and feelings about theology. Why do you feel about it as you do? What are the attitudes of your church or Christian fellowship toward theology?

2. What individuals or groups have contributed most to your own basic understanding of faith? What did you learn from them? Was their influence direct (for example, certain theological ideas) or indirect (basic attitudes)?

3. Is serious theological thought encouraged in your fellowship? (Is the laity trusted?) If not, why not? Are there good reasons for discouraging lay theology?

4. How much of your theology is inherited and how much has been added or at least modified by your own experience as

a Christian? Are there certain points of doctrine on which you differ with many in your denomination? Describe changes in your own religious understanding in the past several years. Can you identify the factors which led to these changes?

5. Are there doctrines or theological teachings of your faith which seem to you of doubtful value or meaning? Why? What doctrines do you find uninteresting? Are there those which you honestly don't understand? Write these down for future reexamination.

6. Write a definition of theology in your own words. Compare it with that of others making the study with you and with the description on page 28 f. Where do these definitions reinforce one another and where do they disagree?

7. Reread pages 29 to 31. Have you really absorbed the meaning of these paragraphs? How does such a description of theology strike you? Are there problems here for your own religious security? If so, why?

8. Were the surprising(?) conclusions on pages 31 to 35 surprising to you?

CHAPTER TWO

Is Theology Necessary?

IF WHAT WE HAVE SAID in the previous chapter is true, why do we need theology at all? If it does not provide us with changeless and infallible knowledge about God, what purpose does it serve? And above all, if one can have a genuine faith and wholesome relation to God despite an inadequate theology, who needs it? Perhaps the "uncultured despisers" of theology are right! In answer to these questions, we may begin by saying that it is doubtful whether theology can be avoided, since it is the intellectual response of the total self to his experience of God. Insofar as a person is mentally sound he reacts to every stimulus as a unity, as a whole self. This means that while some aspects of his experience may not be primarily cognitive or intellectual in character, he still cannot fully appropriate them and make them his without *thinking* about them.

For example, the relationship of a husband and wife is not primarily rational. It did not begin with thought but with sensory encounter ("She was a vision of delight/when first she gleamed upon my sight!"), and it does not normally rest on intellectual but on emotional bonds. But just because the bond of love is real for either partner, they find their whole selves, including their thinking capacities, drawn into the relationship. Love is not thought, but one cannot love without thinking about it. And while the understanding one forms of a loved one and of the relationship of love is never adequate, yet it is a necessary consequence of love.

Similarly, faith is not theology, but one cannot have faith or encounter God without thinking about it. He might avoid theology, on the one hand, by rejecting God, but when God is rejected something else tends to take his place and function as that person's ultimate concern—perhaps it is the state, an economic theory, a system of values—or life tends to lose its unity. And the self-understanding which grows up around this substitute for God (faith has called it an idol) looks suspiciously like theology. This is why value systems such as National Socialism or communism can be spoken of as secular theologies. A believer, on the other hand, might avoid an overt or well-thought-out theology by deliberately suppressing his intellectual response to his faith—by becoming a theological irrationalist—but he would threaten his own personal and mental health without really escaping from theology, because even the judgment that one must not try to think of one's faith is itself a theological judgment.

Theology then is not an option. We are theological if we are disciples. Indeed, if a person responds to God's grace with nothing more than a hallelujah, he has made a beginning of theology. We are *all* theologians; we have no choice in the matter. Our only choice is between a well-thought-out theology and a shoddy and inconsistent one, between good theology and bad. All men, then, have theology. The study of theology is at its best intended to make us more aware of our theological judgments and opinions so that we might more honestly evaluate their correctness and adequacy and so that we might better understand how our theological convictions (and perhaps even our prejudices) influence the way we judge and evaluate the theology of others.

Why Should the Church Have It?

We have not really justified theology simply by showing that it is inescapable. Old age is inescapable, but this is not much to say for it. Does theology serve any positive role in the life of the church? Is it more than a necessary evil? It is not difficult to show that theology has served the church during its history in three positive and important ways. We will look at each briefly:

1. *The church needs theology in order to understand itself.* That is, it needs to clarify its own experience and thought, and to relate its distinctly religious experience to the other areas of experience it shares with the culture of which it is a part. Each of us has at one time or other observed or experienced an event, but lacked the leisure to think about it or its significance. Perhaps it was crowded out of mind by the press of subsequent events. Then later we tried to recapture it, only to find that it was now such a vague memory as to be virtually beyond recall. If, on the other hand, we had been able to stop and reflect while the experience was fresh and to assimilate it into our thoughts, it would have become a relatively clear and permanent element of our lives. Only by thinking about our experiences—by speculating, conceptualizing, relating—do we make them our own, do we nail them down and give them permanent substance.

Similarly our experiences of God and of the church, and the commitments they call forth, demand thought if they are to have substance, clarity and strength. We can really commit to something only if we can say, "Yes, it is true!" and "Yes, I understand it!" and these are rational expressions. We can't even respond to a revelation which is personal and which goes beyond our capacity to verbalize without at least trying to think through what it means. No man can experience without his mind, nor can he be religious without religious thought.

Thus the church has always asked itself questions about its experience of divine revelation and about the faith which results from it, and through the process of asking and answering it has clarified its understanding of what it is as an institution, how it relates to God and the world, what its role is in the world, and what kind of fellowship it should strive to be. Since it finds itself to have come to be through an act of God's grace in Jesus Christ, it has asked about God and also about the Christ in whom that grace has been made known. And through this process, the theological process, the church has come to have a sense of identity, purpose and mission which guides it through history. Many Christians feel no need to think through their faith because they feel they already understand what faith is and who they are. Yet they are already deeply indebted for that understanding to the church and to her theologians who have thought about faith in the past.

Now, since the church is constantly having new experiences and is moving into new periods of history, the need for theology is continuous. With every new cultural development, we in the church must ask anew who we are and what we are to this world. Therefore theology is the never-ending need of the church.

2. The church needs theology in order to define itself. In the sphere of thought and ideas, doctrine is what distinguishes the church from other communities and other systems of ideas. The church is, of course, far more than its doctrine, but its doctrine is very important, for it is the intellectual expression of its inner nature. It is not a matter of indifference what the church believes, because its beliefs express the inner character of its faith. If that inner character changes, it is bound to be reflected in its theology. If its theology becomes vague and poorly wrought, it may express a lack of clarity in the life of the community; it may mean that the church has lost its sense of identity and is in danger of losing its character as the people of God.

This problem of identity probably lies behind the crisis of confidence which has fastened itself on large areas of the church today. The desire of the church to continually broaden its base of service and to deepen its sense of identity with the world—a desire which is certainly motivated by the gospel itself as well as by the needs we see about us—has made it increasingly difficult to distinguish the church from the various other humanitarian activities and expressions of the society. Thus some have come to find the church everywhere—everywhere, that is, but within the organized institutions called by that name.

What exactly is church and what is not? Despite the rightness of the above instincts, it is still true that not everything is the church and not every friendly word is gospel. In the dark, or even in pure light, all distinctions vanish. If the church is everything, then it is nothing. The recognition of this fact is the valid and necessary instinct of the conservative, an instinct which was almost obliterated in the liberal period of Christian theology. For the church to lose its life in service to Christ and to lose its identity as the people of God are not the same.

It is because the church has recognized the danger of losing its identity that it has felt itself compelled from time to time to say no to ideas which it felt would redefine its fundamental nature. These ideas it has usually called "heresy." The distinction between doctrine and heresy is made essential by the need of the church to define itself, to decide what it is and what it is not. Now, this necessity must not make witch hunters of us. Nothing is more tragic than narrow heresy-hunting. There must be room within the grace of God for flexibility and variation in the way we express our faith, but there remains a point where gospel ceases to be gospel. And so there must be an attempt to define what is not gospel, and doctrine is the means by which the church has sought to preserve its identity. Most of the great yeses of Christian affirmation have been born out of challenges to the church which have made it decide what it is not. The history of Christian thought moves forward largely by a dialectic of yes and no, until its true identity, its abiding yes, has been "hardened by the fire of many noes."

3. *The church needs theology in order to communicate itself.* We are a part of a community based on witness. The heart of our faith is bound up in Christ, in whom we believe that God has broken into history for the sake of redemption. Indeed, the meaning of the gospel is contained for us in a series of historical events. Thus the essence of the gospel proclamation, the *kerygma,* is a narration; it is the telling of a story of the mighty acts of God. Now the telling of a story requires the use of language and the conceptual structure which language provides. Proclamation requires words which, even if they are not well-worked-out theology, certainly have theological overtones. So the verbalization of our faith is especially important in a community based on a message which must be communicated. We must remind ourselves again that the encounter with God and the church's response to it are more important than the thought about it, but without thought, the reality of faith becomes incommunicable.

We can thus in summary state our argument in a slightly different way. There are two primary motives which drive the church to theology. The first might be called the *explanatory motive,* by which we seek to state what we believe for our own sake (to understand ourselves), and in which we also seek to state what we believe for the sake of the world (to communicate ourselves). The second is the *protective motive,* by which we seek to preserve the church's existence in the world.

Now, at the risk of becoming tedious, we must again reiterate what has been said before: *theology is not the basis of the community.* We are all a part of this community because we share a common encounter with God through Christ. The way we express this encounter is never perfect, so while you can define Christian ideas in doctrinal terms, *you cannot so define Christians.* We must be continually on guard against saying, "B does not understand the gospel rightly at this point," or "A rejects a certain doctrine," and therefore they cannot be truly Christians. You can never be sure that the theology of a church or a man fully expresses the depth of their commitment.

Why Should You Have a Personal Theology?

It is probably easier to explain to the average Christian why the church should *have* theologians than why he should *be* a theologian. But all that we have said about the character of the church as a community should have begun to make clear the role which the individual plays in the shaping of the church as worship and witness. Most contemporary churches, regardless of their past tradition, have in the present century come to recognize that the church is essentially its people. What Langdon Gilkey has called the victory of the free church tradition in American Christianity has had two wholesome results on the church generally: (1) It has stressed that the church and the people are essentially one. The church is the community, not the hierarchy, the leadership or the denominational structure. Thus if it is to have a living, workable theology it must be because its people individually have wrestled with the task of faith. (2) It has taught us that the pattern of an active ministry and a passive laity is no longer acceptable. We are learning that worship is an active participation of pastor and people in praise and fellowship with God. So also we must learn that the Christian must be active in the struggle to unify modern life under the Spirit of God, and this means theology.

Therefore for the sake of the church, you should be willing to become a theologian. But how about your own needs? From the point of view of your own individual existence as a disciple, why should you have a personal theology? At least three reasons can be briefly mentioned.

1. *To claim your own Christian experience.* Just as the church must appropriate its faith through thought, so the believer can only clarify and claim his own religious experience

by reducing it to words, by thinking on it and speaking of it until it is a conscious part of his past and present. Otherwise, past experiences fade in memory and the present reality of God remains shapeless and vague.

2. *To unite all of your life under the grace of God.* The Greek word *soteria*, translated in the English New Testament by "salvation," often carried the suggestion of "bodily health and safety," or, one might say, "wholeness." Both the Latin *salvatio* and the German *heil* from *heilen* ("heal, make whole") reflect this same meaning. To be saved is to be healed, made whole, unified. While wholeness does not exhaust the meaning of salvation, it does make clear that the experience of grace should have the effect of healing the brokenness of our lives and of putting an end to the self-destructive warfare of the soul which flesh is heir to. While once again this healing takes place in its fundamental sense at a more basic level than thought, yet it is a sound theology which helps the believer to unite warring values and to bring his thinking about God, self and the world together into a wholeness of thought which is a part of the wholeness of the Spirit.

3. *To relate your faith to the challenges of modern life.* Since faith aims at unifying life, at making us whole, then the Christian in the world must seek to understand his faith in the light of the rapidly changing situation of that world. He must also seek to understand his world in the light of his faith. He cannot countenance the spiritual schizophrenia so common in the church which tries to isolate the religious from the secular. There cannot be in our century any "six days and Sunday." And the understanding of what it means to be a Christian in a changing world—and more important, what it means to be the particular Christian that *you are*— is a most important function of your personal theology.

Indeed, the breathtaking rate of change in our century makes a living personal theology more critical than ever before. It has sometimes been said in previous times that it took two generations for theological change to be felt in the church, one generation to move from the theologians to the parish ministers and another to filter down to the layman. But this oxcart process simply cannot be allowed anymore. Today there is no time. The world will not wait for our leisure. If the church is to have any word for our world, it must be because those of us who live daily the life of change live also daily the life of theology.

One of the most refreshing aspects of the current crisis of the church is the emergence of a new, alert, sometimes argumentative and rebellious, but concerned group of lay theologians, most of whom are hammering out their faith not in the traditional cloister, but in the labs, the ghettos, the suburbs where they live and breathe. To say that they can or should replace the scholar or the professional, whose broader preparation and perspective give him a peculiar opportunity to act as moderator and synthesizer, would be undoubtedly wrong. But it would be right, I think, to say that if the church is to have a future theology, it must bear the marks of these "soldier theologians" to a degree never before true in Christian history. The layman is certain to lead more decisively in shaping the church, its worship, and its thought in the future than he has ever done in the past, and the invitation to develop a personal theology is an invitation to share in this future.

Developing Theological Sensitivity and Taste

Theologians sometimes argue with one another concerning whether theology can properly be considered a science. Insofar as it seeks to deal with a unified body of experience in an orderly fashion, it can perhaps be called in the broadest sense a science. However, as with all those areas of human thought that try to look at life more or less as a whole and to give expression to that whole—literature, philosophy, ethics—it partakes also of the quality of an art. And while certain skills are required for theology to be done in the most adequate way, equally important are the sensitivity and capacity for penetrating to the heart of language and experience which characterize the greatest literary and artistic minds.

I have often been impressed by the almost instinctive perception and understanding which mark the great theologians of the church. Men such as Augustine, Luther, Schleiermacher and Tillich seem to possess a natural feeling for the deep questions which well up in the hearts of men as they experience birth, temptation, death and beauty—as they gaze into the "windows to the infinite." This sensitivity to the pulse of the human soul is no doubt what made them great theologians and gave them their peculiar power to move us to understanding. Yet few of us are without some measure of these qualities which are, after all, expressions of our fundamental humanity, and they can most surely be refined and sharpened by our efforts and by God's grace.

I will mention at this point only three elements of theological taste which we must seek to cultivate if the personal theology which we try to create is to be wholesome and redemptive in us and toward others, as well as intellectually respectable:

1. *Learning to respect all men.* It should go without saying that no adequate theology can grow out of narrowness or hostility toward other groups, ideologies, or theologies. Such a theology will bear the marks of its origin. It will be one-sided, disruptive and spiritually destructive to the group or sect that owns it. Yet such are our backgrounds and such are our insecurity and sin that we find it extremely difficult to respect all men and to learn from those who differ from us.

Only gradually does a Christian learn to master his native fear and to begin to trust others and to listen to them. But we are not without resources to help us in this process. We have already learned to distinguish between men and their doctrines, and this should allow us a greater range of compassion. We have also confessed that our own theology is not infallible and is never fully adequate, and this confession of humility should help us to listen as well as speak. And finally, the conviction that we live before God by forgiveness should deliver us from the compulsive desire for certainty and make possible a new openness to others and to God.

2. *Learning to be sensitive to the real meanings.* I am an amateur ornithologist of many years' standing, and frequently I amaze my friends by detecting, sometimes in the midst of city noise, bird sounds that they not only did not notice but couldn't hear when I called their attention to them. My hearing is not exceptional, but it has by years of listening been attuned to catch the subtle notes of a warbler or a vireo in the live oaks which escape others' notice.

In a similar but more demanding way a person can cultivate a kind of spiritual keenness of hearing, or a sensitivity to meanings that permits him to go behind the language with which people speak and detect the real intentions—the questions, the fears, the hopes, the experiences of worship, the ecstasy, the agony which always rise so haltingly to expression. It is to the credit of contemporary theology that it has struggled so hard to encourage and develop this sensitivity. One of the most wholesome facts of twentieth-century Christianity is the movement of Christians toward one another in a new kind of unity of spirit; and theology—so long a divisive influence in Christendom—has been one of the most powerful forces in this move toward unity, chiefly because it has begun to find the deep currents of common faith which unite us by learning to search for the real meanings.

The Christian theolog must seek to listen and to find what is real and valid in the least attractive expression of faith. And he can be sure that any tenet held with any degree of passion by any Christian is not without its real religious value, however obscure it may be to his own hearing. He must learn to listen to the past also, and in so doing he will often be surprised to learn that the obscure and meaningless doctrines which have been handed down to the present and which seem so irrelevent to life today are still rich with power and meaning. He must listen with the same sympathy to every critic and enemy of faith—atheist, Communist, humanist—in order that he might understand and share their doubts and hopes, for then he can learn to speak to them. When we have learned to listen, we are near to being theologians.

3. *The art of recasting and translating.* The theologian is a mediator. By his calling (as disciple) and by his discipline (as theologian) he stands between God and his own soul, between the church and world, between brother and brother. And he mediates by translating—that is, by earnestly listening and then by interpreting one to another. He helps each to understand the other and therefore he is a peacemaker.

I am surprised at how often I find myself playing the role of the interpreter, and trying to lead my students to translate strange ideas or unfamiliar theology into the language of their own experience. By such translation they often find common ground for faith with the holders of such theology. And the lay theologian will seek to put his newly developed skill in hearing to the task of bringing men together in understanding. He is also a mediator between past and present, for it is his task to interpret the great doctrinal heritage of the past, to recast and reexpress it so as to reveal its depth and universality and its abiding power. And by doing this he reunites the church of our day, which like so much in our culture seems to be losing contact with its roots and suffering as a result of a kind of spiritual vertigo, with the solid foundation on which it rests in the church of the past and above all in the incarnation of God in Christ.

SUGGESTIONS FOR THOUGHT
AND DISCUSSION

1. Which of the motives for theology (for example, the explanatory or the protective) is strongest in your church or faith?

2. List some of the theological teachings or ideas that you

consider false or dangerous (that is, heresies) and try to say why you feel this way. Do they threaten or deny something important to you? What? Do they threaten the identity of the church? How?

3. Try this group experiment: Let one or more persons attempt to express the meaning of their faith in pantomime. How essential are words to communication? Even if the attempt is reasonably successful, was it because certain symbols or actions used had meanings which were shared by the group (like cross, resurrection, death, etc.)?

4. The author asserts (p. 44) that a personal theology should help to heal and unify your life under God. Has your theology in the past had a healing and unifying influence on your life or has it generated conflict and disruption? Can you single out elements of conflict (for example, conflict over election and free will, or God's love and judgment)? Ask the same questions of your church's theology.

5. Are there points of tension between your faith and the outlooks and attitudes you share as a modern person? Bring them out in the open and discuss them.

6. Concerning theological sensitivity and taste: Write down some theological doctrine or idea with which you disagree. Then wrestle with it and see if you can speculate on why those who hold this idea feel it is important. What are they trying to affirm?

PART TWO

At the Getting Place

(The Sources and Norms of Theology)

CHAPTER THREE

The Dialogue of Faith

IN THE PREVIOUS DISCUSSION we have been laying a very general groundwork for theology, with special attention to establishing the motives for and purposes of personal theology. In the present part of our study we will seek to do three things. First, we will introduce the reader to the various resources on which he may draw in constructing his own understanding of faith; second, we will try to describe the way in which these resources enrich and also regulate one another; finally, we will suggest some goals or standards against which the believer should continually measure and validate his own theology.

When I was a boy, my parents had ways of turning aside the too-persistent questions of which I was always full. If I asked about the source of anything (from bicycles to babies) which they could not or preferred not to divulge, they would reply, half-facetiously, "Where do you get that? Why, at the getting place!" This is the question we must now ask and seek to answer. Where does one, after all, get theology? I am tempted to answer, "At the getting place," in order to forestall the oversimplified and often misleading answers to which we are accustomed. As you are no doubt learning by now, nothing in theology is quite as simple as it may have in the past seemed. But this is because life is not simple, and we reduce it to simple formulas only by suppressing its dynamism and its vitality. Theology is born out of a dialogue in which many persons and many aspects of experience play a part. We must now try to understand the nature of this dialogue and the part the theologian plays in it.

The Dynamic Character of Faith

Since it is a commitment of the whole life to God, the life of faith partakes of the rich and constantly growing complex of relations and experience which constitutes this totality of life. This means that theology, as our attempt to understand and unify life in relation to God, is influenced by every element of experience, and that like life, it is also dynamic. In fact, theology grows out of the interplay of the different dimensions of life. It seeks to hear what each of these dimensions has to say about what it means to be a man and a believer. Therefore each becomes a member of a continuing "dialogue." Now such a picture of theology as being in essence dialogic is in contrast to the picture presented in some forms of traditional theology.

Often theology is understood as resulting from a kind of monologue between God and man, in which God speaks, either directly and personally through his Spirit or indirectly through prophet, Bible or church, and man receives. Here the sole content of doctrine is from God and the entire role of man is to passively accept, and perhaps be grateful. But an understanding of doctrine as the content of such a divine monologue is unacceptable for at least two reasons:

(1) It simply is not true to the facts of history. It is easy to demonstrate that the more or less officially accepted doctrine of any group has gone through a history of change, and that its particular shape has been influenced by many factors, cultural, social, and historical. While not denying that there

may be a real "word from the Lord" at the heart of such a theology, we can see clearly that the shaping of its final form was influenced by many things other than that word. (2) Such a viewpoint, by rejecting any sources of influence other than God, must necessarily identify its own dogma with absolute and infallible truth and reject every other kind of theological thought as false and demonic. Not only does such a position have difficulty explaining its own changing history, but it tends to produce a kind of religious narrowness which is intolerant of any difference and destructive of the true fruits of the Spirit. On the other hand, an understanding of doctrine as growing out of the life situation of the church and of the Christian is in keeping with the actual experience of history and need not repudiate other theologies or interpretations of faith. It can receive them as members of the dialogue of faith.

But What about God?

Most of the traditional Christian communities in the West assume that in some sense the source of theology is God. Christianity is a religion of revelation. We assume that man is not by himself capable of achieving an adequate or redemptive knowledge of God unless God reveals himself to man. Furthermore, all true knowledge of ourselves is possible only in the light of grace, which is to say by God's gracious self-manifestation. How then do we square this with the above suggestion that the sources of theology are more than one and that they are not all God? To this question we must answer the following: (1) Insofar as God is creator as well as redeemer, God is manifest in some respect in all things. Although theologians differ on the value and function of "natural revelation," they usually agree that nothing is excluded in principle as a source of revelation, since God can become manifest to the believer in all things he has made. "The heavens declare the glory of God; and the firmament showeth his handiwork." (2) Insofar as we are men (and

therefore incapable of the infinite), sinners (and therefore
incapable of perfect comprehension) and social beings
(therefore experiencing all things through our social existence), we ordinarily encounter God in and through the
objects, events, institutions and relationships of our corporate and natural existence. Indeed, some theologians would
say that our experience of God is never direct, but is always
mediated. It may be mediated by an institution (the church),
an object or event (a burning bush, a crossing of the sea,
a sacrament), a sacred book or document (the Bible), but
it is always mediated. Even when the experience is a direct
and personal one with no book, object or event involved, it
is still received in and mediated by our own personhood, so
that while we believe that we can distinguish God's presence
and grace from the human emotion that accompanies it,
yet they can never be separated. Israel became aware of this
situation when it sought to be the people of God. In principle, Israel was ruled directly by God and had no king but
him. This they affirmed at Sinai and reaffirmed each year by
covenant renewal. But in actual fact, when one sought God
to know his will, he always met some human figure, such as
a priest, a king, a prophet, or some sacred object, such as
the Urim and the Thummin. This hiddenness of God both
comforted Israel with the assurance of his divine majesty
and perplexed her with the elusiveness of his truth.

Thus, while the theologian is assured that finally all knowledge *does* come from God, yet God confronts us in many
ways, and potentially any moment of experience may become filled with his presence. Thus there are in principle as
many sources of theology as there are elements and moments
of experience. We meet God in and through his world.

Members of the Dialogue

In actual historical experience, not all elements or moments of experience are equally sources of the knowledge of

God, and therefore of theology, at least insofar as it is Christian theology. God could in principle confront us anywhere and therefore the raw material of theology might be provided in the most unexpected places. However, it has been generally the case that Christian theology has grown out of dialogue between four primary and closely interdependent sources. Theology has usually been born out of the creative tension between (1) the revelation of God in Christ himself, (2) in the Scriptures, (3) in the church as the community of faith and the creation of God's Spirit, and (4) in the heart of the individual through forgiveness and regeneration. These are the members of the dialogue and they will prove to be the great sources out of which your theology, if it is Christian and if it is personal, will largely be drawn. The issues that confront you as you seek to understand your faith will invariably drive you to ask these four questions:

1. What did Christ teach, or what does he say on the matter?
2. What say the Scriptures?
3. What have Christians (the church) believed?
4. What does my own experience bear witness to?

Every serious expression of the Christian faith has been an attempt to bring together the testimony of each of these "moments of revelation," and every great theology has sought to draw deeply and appropriately from each and to hold them together in creative tension. And your personal theology must give evidence of this tension.

Now in this catalog of the sources of doctrine it is clear that Christ himself has a priority. To be Christian means no less than the acceptance that the final revelation of God is in Jesus. It is a matter of debate whether and to what extent we are to seek that finality of authority propositionally in what he taught or experientially in what has happened in the church and in us through him. In other words, it is not merely as prophet but as creator of the church and

redeemer that we call him Christ. But in either case, while
in principle Christ is the final source for faith (and in the
sense described below, also the final norm), yet in actual
experience we have no point of contact with Christ except
through the other members of the dialogue. If we wish to
know what Christ taught on a matter we must go to Scripture. If we wish to say what it is that Christ has done in the
world we must look at the church or probe our own sense
of redemption. So in practical experience, the primary sources
on which we find ourselves continually drawing are the three
remaining, namely, Scripture, church and individual experience.

This then is the fundamental answer to the first of the
two decisive questions for theology, namely: "Where do we
go for the stuff of our theology?" The answer is "To Christ,
first of all and finally, and then to the Scriptures, to the
living community of the church, and lastly to the confirmation of the Holy Spirit in our Christian life."

But there is a second decisive question (and finally there
are no others), namely, "How do we choose?" There is so
much in Scripture and church, so many varieties of opinions
claiming our allegiance, and so many conflicting instincts
arising from our own psyches. In other words, we need not
only *sources* from which to draw our theology but *norms* or
standards to regulate us, to keep us from going astray or
being misled by whims or prejudices. Where are we to find
these norms? In actual experience, we have usually found
our regulating norms for theology in the sources. In other
words, the four great sources of Christian life, Christ, the
Scriptures, the church, and the experience of the believer
function not only as sources but also as checks upon one
another, so that if one is tempted to build too exclusively
on one source, with the danger of a distortion, he finds his
error called into question by the others. This is what we
mean when we speak of the dialogue of faith, and when we
say that the sources exist in tension with one another.

Probably no theology has ever been completely balanced, that is, has drawn equally from each source. There are many reasons why this is so. One generation of theologians may draw too exclusively from one source, so that emphasis on another becomes dominant in subsequent generations as a corrective. This is what happened in the sixteenth century when Reformation theology, in revolt against too complete dependence of medieval theology on the traditions of the church, adopted as its slogan *sola scriptura,* "Scripture only," and again in the nineteenth century when classic liberalism, in reaction to a narrow and excessive biblicism, emphasized the religious experience of the believer. But by and large, these overemphases on one source over against the others are usually balanced by the broader experience of the church. Each calls the other in question and acts as a balance or compensation. The members of the dialogue would better be called not simply sources, but *source-norms,* to express this dual function which they perform in the life of faith.

The way in which each of these source-norms functions in the church can be seen by the way it operates to enrich and yet to regulate and correct the thought of the individual Christian. So long as he remains rooted in the life of the church, he cannot escape the gnawing questions which arise from his own mind when he is tempted to ignore one or more of these sources of Christian doctrine.

For example, suppose he has a flash of personal insight to the effect that God loves only Aryans. If this impression is strong enough he may be tempted to introduce it as a tenet of his theology. But insofar as he is sane *and* Christian, he may have doubts about such a tenet. He will wonder if he really has the right to adopt such a dogma, or having adopted it to call it Christian. After all, has anybody in the church ever really believed this? He may ask, "Can this be Christian just because *I* say so? Am I not *required* to test this insight against all the past generations of Christians? Is it possible that I alone have the Christian truth and everybody else is

out of step?" He will also wonder whether he should not
search the Scriptures. If he finds no passage which can reasonably be interpreted in support of his conviction, he will
become increasingly unsure of himself. If finally he wonders
how Jesus would have felt about his opinion, and suspects
that Jesus would have not been a "respecter of persons" or
of races, then he will find it very difficult indeed to hold to
his conviction concerning Aryans or to propagate it with any
confidence of success in the church. He will probably conclude that he was mistaken, or cling to his position and
become increasingly alienated from the Christian community,
for a conclusion that Christ, the Scriptures and the church
were wrong is virtually a rejection of Christianity as the
governing commitment of his life.

In the above example, one can see how one source, personal experience, was called into question and tested by the
others, the church, the Scriptures, and Christ. Thus by
raising their voices as true and proper expressions of Christian
faith the latter serve as norms to regulate the former. The
choice could have been otherwise. Too great a dependence
on the church ("What *has* the church said or what *is* it
saying?") may call us to ask, "But could the church be
wrong here? What do the Scriptures say?" Suppose the church
has discriminated against a minority and has justified such
discrimination by doctrine (for example, persecution of Jews
on the grounds that as a people they carry the guilt of
murdering Jesus). Can it be squared with the teachings of
Scripture? Can it be squared with the admonitions of my
Christian conscience which has learned through grace that
God loves all men equally? Too narrow and uncritical a
biblicism may also be challenged and examined by the word
of the church and in the light of Christian experience. And
so our Christian theology is born out of this living exchange
between these three critical focuses of its life.

Now, it is important to understand that I am not trying
to say how theology *ought* to be done in proposing this

three-pole, "dialogic" theory. Good theory should reflect and describe conditions as they exist. Thus I am describing how it has been done throughout Christian history and how it must be done. All Christian theology, when it is truly Christian and truly personal, not just a fifth generation hand-me-down, has come out of such a dialogue, whether it has been thoroughly and consistently carried out or not, and whether the resulting theology is adequate or complete. Our purpose is to make the process conscious so that it may function more consistently and creatively in your attempts to develop a personal and usable Christian faith.

I think it is fair to say that all of these source-norms are present in some degree in every Christian communion. But in most fellowships one of them will tend to dominate, and this dominant element will be largely responsible for the distinctive quality or character of that fellowship and of its theology. Thus in Christian history it has usually been possible to distinguish certain types of churches, for example, the "church-type" (Roman and Orthodox Catholicism), the "biblical-type" (Calvinism, most characteristically) and the so-called "spiritualist-sectarian type" (Quaker, and other Anabaptist groups). Nor is such a dominance of one source-norm necessarily a bad thing, for each community by its special emphasis contributes to the richness and variety of Christian theology, and each one contributes its natural feeling for an element of Christian experience which might otherwise be neglected. For example, my own fellowship has a keen feeling for the Scriptures, drawing as it does from its roots in Reformation theology. It also has roots in the spiritualism of Sectarian or Anabaptist Christianity, and therefore has some sense of the place of personal experience as a source of doctrine. But because both Reformation and Sectarian Christianity were revolts against an excessive "churchism," my own people have been left with a somewhat deficient sensitivity to God's action within the historic community, that is, within Christian tradition. The two Catholic communities, however, and to some extent the Lutheran, have preserved this feeling for the church—for that great company of the past which we can never escape and to which we are responsible as the living present of God's grace. Thus by learning from these church-type churches my own group may be led to recover a feeling for the church and may be warned away from too great a dominance of our life and thought by the other source-norms.

The dangers of the dominance of one source-norm in our understanding are mainly two: First, we may be led to distort the content of faith and to neglect important elements of truth, thus ending in a lopsided theology. Second, we may become dishonest, wishing to so strongly stress our own norm (e.g., the Bible) that we may end by denying that there are any other sources at work in us, or that they deserve a hearing at all. And we may therefore become subject to innumerable subtle influences, not all of them wholesome or Christian, while deceiving ourselves that they are the voice of Scripture, church, or Holy Spirit.

Thus the picture we have presented of the development of theology is one of faith in tension between these primary pivots of its existence. Theology must draw from and conform to the revelation of God in Christ and his church, else it is not *Christian*. It must draw from and be confirmed by the believer's experience of faith and life, else it is not *his own*. Now, such a picture is certainly more complex than some of the views of authority which are commonly encountered in book and pulpit. But while simplicity is a consummation devoutly to be wished, it must not be achieved by an oversimplification which is not true to the facts and which can finally lead us into all manner of theological and religious sins. I am aware, for example, that such a picture lacks the directness of a kind of biblical exclusivism still popular in some circles, which claims to draw all its insights on faith from Scripture alone, quite oblivious to the manner in which church, cultural and family attitudes have shaped its interpretation of the Scripture. Thus by losing something of the directness and simplicity of exclusive biblicism it also escapes to a degree its penchant for self-deception.

Such a view may lose something also in a certain kind of assurance. Dogmatism (whether church dogmatism or Bible dogmatism) is welcomed by many because they feel a need for a firm authority. Such people are apt to feel that a theology in constant tension and development deprives them of the certainty which they seek in faith. While we may agree that certainty is desirable, we must object that faith in *theology* or even in one (or all) of the source-norms of theology is a misplaced faith and is likely one day to crumble under the pressure of experience. Our faith is not in theology or even in the source-norms we have described, but in God! Furthermore, what we lose in simplicity and in a kind of certainty by such a view of authority, we gain in flexibility, honesty, balance and humility.

Understanding and Exploring the Sources

We have been describing what we have called the primary source-norms for theology, and have implied that these are in the broadest sense the answers to the fundamental theological questions, "What can we say?" and "How can we decide?" We need now to take a closer look at each in order to understand the role which it plays as source and norm for theology, and to suggest how the Christian can begin to employ its insights in the shaping of his own theology.

A word of warning is in order here, because in the following discussion we must come to grips with more specific theological concepts than has been hitherto the case. Therefore my own theological views on Scripture, the church and the Christian life will be more difficult to keep out of the discussion. The reader is under no obligation to make these his own. My hope is that where *my* personal theology intrudes, he will either find it reasonable and persuasive or will use it as an anvil for beating out a position which will be his own.

SUGGESTIONS FOR THOUGHT
AND DISCUSSION

1. Make a list of some of the people, experiences, groups, books, movies, art works, etc., which have influenced your own ways of thinking about life and God. How many of these were directly church-related or "religious" influences?

2. Examine the four sources and norms for theology described on pages 56–64. What importance has each had in your background and church? If your church stresses, for example, the Scriptures, does it have informal or unwritten traditions which influence its theology? How well is the tension between the source-norms maintained?

3. Chapter 2 sets forth a "doctrine" of authority. How well does it describe the actual situation in the life of the church as you experience it? Do you see any advantages in this three-fold understanding of authority? Do you see any problems?

CHAPTER FOUR

The Scriptures

EVERY CHRISTIAN COMMUNITY and every Christian theology recognize that the Scriptures hold a special place as source and norm for faith. But the exact place and authority of Scripture vary widely from church to church and even within a church or denomination. Between the Catholic and non-Catholic churches there has even been a difference of opinion concerning the content of Scriptures. Furthermore, the degree and character of the authority given to Scripture has been affected by changing historical circumstances.

It is probably true that most previous centuries have allowed the Bible a wider range of authority and a more decisive role in shaping, not only theology proper, but their understanding of nature, life and ethics as well, than is the case in the present century. Indeed, it would probably be safe to say that the question of the authority of Scriptures has undergone a rather complete reexamination in the last century and a half. It is also true that faith in the reliability or the adequacy of Scripture is going through a crisis in contemporary life. This is as true for those who still profess a doctrine of infallibility and defend the absolute authority of Scripture as it is for those who do not. This crisis grows out of the fact that the whole understanding of the universe has changed radically in the past three centuries. The world view of the first century A.D., in which the New Testament came to life and which so deeply shaped the language and thought of the biblical writers, is no longer that of modern men. And this is true not only of the religious or theological liberal; it is true of every modern man.

We do not choose our world view; it is not an option but a given fact. Thus one of the critical questions facing the Christian theologian today is that of understanding how the Scriptures, which were conceived and written in a different world, can be meaningful and powerful for our own. Are there respects in which we can and must admit that Scripture is limited or not authoritative? Are there ways in which it can be translated or reinterpreted into the vernacular of our world so that it can speak with power?

It seems doubtful that any modern man can look upon the Scriptures as a valid and reliable authority in matters scientific as did medieval Christians. Beginning with Copernicus, scientific study has created a view of the world which is both different from the biblical world view and for us absolutely authoritative. In place of a relatively small, world-centered universe created in a moment only a few millennia ago, we now are confronted by an inconceivably vast universe which has come into being in an almost equally vast time span. And although many of us are made most uncomfortable by such a world, and especially by what it implies about man's place and value in that world, we can't really escape it. Those who continue to carry on a rear guard action against geology and evolution can't conceal from us the fact that our children have no choice about the matter. For them and for all future generations some form of developmentalism will be not theory but fact, and not a conclusion but a starting point.

Furthermore, we all *live* by this new view, whether we

like to admit it or not, as witnessed by the fact that the most conservative theologian consults a geologist and not the Scriptures when he wants to dig for oil. At every practical level we accept the sovereignty of the scientific picture of the world. This is borne out by the fact that even when we seek to "harmonize" science and Scripture we usually seek to show that Scripture really doesn't disagree with science, rather than the reverse. Nor can we any longer take refuge in the minor disagreements of scientists or their frequent revisions of their theories, for it is the practical effectiveness of their basic theory which enables them to broaden and modify the details with confidence. For example, while biologists may disagree on the details of evolution or the mechanisms at work in it, there is no disagreement on the principle of biological development. Evolution is not theory to modern scientists, it is fact. Nor is it less than fact to a whole generation of school children for whom the Scopes trial in Tennessee cannot be seen as anything other than a page from a comic opera. Clarence Darrow did not need to win his case. Time and the cumulative effects of research have won it for him. The disparity between Genesis and Darwin, if it comes down to it, has really been decided for all of us in Darwin's favor.

If the Scriptures are not then reliable in matters scientific, how can they be trusted in other matters? Furthermore, scientific ("critical") study of the Scriptures has made clear the very human quality of the Bible itself, and has shown the rather surprising variety of outlook, witness, opinion and theology to be found in the Bible. What does this say about its authority? If indeed this book is shot-through with humanity, how can it be relied on as a testimony to faith and a source of doctrine?

These and other related problems have led many Christians in the last century and a half to reexamine the nature and character of scriptural authority, or to develop a new doctrine of Scripture more commensurate with the modern world view. Now whether the reader agrees with the above judgments or himself feels that the authority of Scripture in these matters has been called into question, we must insist that those who felt these problems to be real were not simply weak or malicious men, seeking to destroy faith by their re-examinations. On the contrary, they sought to face the problems confronting biblical faith because they believed in its basic truth and were willing to seek for answers.

Nevertheless the shock of the nineteenth century to the collective nervous system of faith was considerable. It did shatter the older and often comfortable securities of the age of faith. Yet the very crisis of Scripture has proved to be at least in part a blessing, for it has driven Christian thinkers to reexamine the Scriptures, and to ask new questions about the nature and extent of its authority and truth, and to point us in new and fruitful directions. It is no accident that the biblical critical movement of the nineteenth century led to a biblically centered theology in the first half of the twentieth in theologians such as Karl Barth, Emil Brunner, Reinhold Niebuhr, and Paul Tillich.

Understanding the Nature and Authority of the Scriptures

Many (though not all) of our problems in hearing and understanding the Bible arise not from the nature of the Bible itself, but from our ideas about the Bible—in other words, from our *theology* of the Bible. If we attribute to the Scriptures a kind of power or authority which they never claimed or needed and then they turn out not to possess such a power, it is not the Scriptures which have proved false but our theology of Scripture. If, for instance, I make of the Bible a magic amulet or charm, and it does not protect me from injury, then the Scripture cannot be blamed. Yet the authority of Scripture has become so closely identified for many with the theological idea of "infallibility" or "factual inerrancy" that many feel that they must give up the Bible altogether when they can no longer accept the dogma of inerrancy.

The first step for many in developing a personal theology is to rethink the nature and character of biblical authority, asking, "What do honesty and common sense require me to affirm? What actual power and authority can the Bible have for my life? How does the Bible as a source of faith relate to the other source-norms of faith?" Perhaps even more basically, "What sort of a book is it after all?" The answers to the questions must finally be your own, but I can point out for your consideration certain ways of looking at the Bible which seem to me preliminary to any workable doctrine of Scripture for our time:

1. *We need to understand the Bible as a creation of faith.* The Scriptures were born out of the believing community. The Catholic authorities say that the church created the Bible, and historically they are correct. This tells us something about the purposes behind its creation. It was the product of religious faith. It was written by a religious community (or communities) in order to express and communicate their faith and its meaning to their children and to those who would listen.

Now while the purpose of the Bible was religious, it necessarily had to be written in the language and the thought patterns of its day. What other language did they have at their disposal? Since its various writers, Hebrew and Greek, were men living in the physical world, they could not avoid couching their thoughts in the world view, even in the primitive science of their day. Yet it was not their purpose or their chief concern to comment on cosmology or physics any more than a poet or a preacher expects his random or descriptive references to nature to be drawn out of their literary or homiletic context and set up as criteria of natural truth for all ages. On such matters they did not (and did not intend to) speak as authorities but as men who took for granted the common opinions of their day.

They had a somewhat deeper interest in history than they

had in astronomy or physics because Hebrew and Christian alike saw history as the arena of God's redemptive work. But their concern was not in the disinterested examination of past events. They were not antiquarians. Their interest in history was a concern for bearing witness to the acts of God within it. Thus their history is "prejudiced." Biblical writers not only write what happened but they interpret it in the light of faith. In fact, they might even on occasion rearrange or modify the facts so as to make clear the religious meaning.

The facts were for them nothing unless they testified to the gracious, loving and redemptive Lord of history. Their purpose was not to inform or to report but to *bear witness*. And one cannot begin to understand the clearly provable inadequacies of Scripture scientifically and historically, or its peculiar richness and power to move men to worship and to repentance unless he takes this purpose seriously. The Old Testament is not science or history; it is *confession* to the marvelous grace of God who called Israel forth to be his people. At the heart of the Old Testament is an event which must be confessed ("A wandering Aramean was my father . . . and the Lord heard our voice . . . and brought us out of Egypt with a mighty hand."), and proclaimed ("Hear, O Israel, the Lord is one!"). So also at the heart of the New Testament is an event to be confessed ("God . . . who called you out of darkness into his marvelous light") and witnessed to ("God has made him both Lord and Christ.").

Our first step then in discovering what kind of authority the Scripture can have for today and in developing an adequate doctrine of Scripture is to learn to listen to the Bible for what it is, a book of witness and of faith, in order that we might hear what it seeks to say and what it is really *able* to say. The proper reaction to a word of witness and confession is not assent but response. Somehow we must find the real power and value of Scripture in its word of confession and proclamation. It speaks the language of faith and its real authority is an authority of faith.

2. *We need to understand that, like every living thing, the Scripture grew!* That is, it was not given to Israel and the church as a single document perfectly conceived and executed by the hand of God. It grew as the experience of Israel with God grew and matured, and it grew as the early church grew in its experience of God in Christ. There are religions which teach that their sacred documents were handed down intact from heaven untouched, so to speak, by human hands. Christians have sometimes been tempted to understand the Bible this way.

I recall the college friend who one night in the dormitory defended the position that after Paul had written Romans he had to read it to see what it said. I was reminded of the painting which is alleged to have hung in a German monastery. It pictured a bearded scribe at a desk with pen in hand. The writer was clearly unconscious or asleep, while behind him stood an angel who over his shoulder guided the pen. The painting was called "Inspiration." Both illustrations imply the absence of any human experience or personality in Scripture and therefore deny any real human history to it. The Hebrew-Christian tradition as a whole has never sought to make such a claim, because such a view is inappropriate and unworthy of the dynamism of the biblical faith. Thus we are under no obligation, as are those who hold such views, to explain away the obvious evidences of growth through human experience in the Scriptures.

While the Bible is the book of God, it is also the book of Israel and the book of the church. It is a living book of human experience born out of a living community. It is saturated with the personalities not only of the men who wrote the individual works it contains, but with the corporate personality of the community of faith from which it comes. The authors and compilers of the Bible clearly understood this when they affixed the names of its authors to its divisions. The Bible may be a writing through which God speaks, but David also speaks through it as does Paul.

Now such a dynamic view of Scripture is in harmony with our understanding of theology as a living product of Christian life and experience, but more important, it prepares us to recognize without fear two facts about the Bible which more rigid views may obscure or even drive us to deny. First is the rich diversity of the biblical writings. These texts tell us of God but they also tell us of the people. Now, we don't mean merely literary variety (poetry, prophecy, etc.) or cultural variety (Egyptian customs, Greek customs, etc.). It is also clear that we have *theological* variety in the Scriptures, as each prophet or apostolic writer bears witness to his faith in God and his knowledge of God in terms of his own experience and understanding. In other words, we have the "personal theology" of Amos, Jeremiah, Isaiah, Luke, John and many others in Scripture. And once we have recognized the living character of the Bible, we are no longer under any compulsion to deny this variety. We can accept it joyfully and see how it enriches our total picture of Christ and of God as revealed in Scripture.

Now if it is objected that theological variety destroys the unity of the Scriptures, we must ask, "Does the variety of personal faith within a church destroy its unity?" Not so long as there is a common experience of God and a common sense of forgiveness. This is the cement of the fellowship which encourages and makes possible personal uniqueness and honest expression. There is abundant evidence that in ancient Israel and in the Apostolic church there were differences and even disagreements, but all such were within the common life of the Spirit. Why should we not expect the writings which record their experience with God to reflect this difference in unity which marked the believing community?

The second fact which we are now ready to recognize is that of development. The Scriptures reflect the growing ex-

perience of men with God. Therefore we can expect their
own slow maturing in faith to be evidenced. And this is so.
The Christian is already prepared for the fact of development by his belief that the Old Testament, though truly
from God, is neither so clear, complete or adequate as the
New Testament. Thus we have usually agreed there is growth
of understanding from Old Covenant to New. This is what
we mean when we accept the Old Testament as truly Scripture but interpret it in the light of the New Testament and
of Christ. Thus we give tacit consent to a difference in
authority or adequacy between the testaments. We need
now to recognize different degrees of adequacy and fullness
of understanding *within* the testaments. We would have no
trouble recognizing this fact were it not for the idea of "equal
inspiration" often associated with some of the more rigid
views of the Scripture. This doctrine maintains that all parts
of Scripture are equally inspired and authoritative for faith.
But such views, far from helping to strengthen the authority
of Scripture, have eroded it away by calling on people to
accept as equally binding differing and sometimes deeply
troubling passages.

For example, my Christian students who have learned
to see God through the eyes of Isaiah and Jesus Christ have
a great moral difficulty with Joshua's tactics at Jericho and
Ai. How can one who takes Christ seriously believe that the
slaughter of the Jericho children really pleased God? If Jesus
says the Kingdom is of little children and Joshua has them
slain in the name of God, how can we hold these to be
equally authoritative? The subterfuges we create to avoid
the problem (for example, the analogy of "radical surgery")
don't really solve it, but usually leave us with the guilty
feeling that we have evaded the issue. But can we not agree
that Joshua, a most sincere and devout man, led Israel at a
time when she had not yet reached the mature understanding
implied by her calling? Surely God had made himself known
at Sinai as the God of creation and therefore of all men

(even Canaanites), but it was a long time before the full implications of his calling and of his character would become clear. It is a long way from the first Joshua to the last. (Joshua and Jesus both mean "Savior.") We can recognize that God used Joshua's imperfect leadership to move Israel toward his future redemptive purpose, but we need not insist that everything Joshua thought or did represents the perfect truth or will of God. And the examples could be multiplied endlessly. Is Abraham's example of faith equally a guide for Christian conscience when he "believes God" and when he indulges in multiple wives?

Since the New Testament was written in the full light of the cross and the resurrection, we will not find there such great differences of outlook. Nevertheless, the early Christians also had to pioneer in faith. They had to take the realities of Easter and Pentecost and work out their meaning for the church. Again the results show a growing understanding from the first halting efforts in Acts to the mature theologies of Paul, Luke, and John. And again this growth points us to the living nature of the New Testament and of the community which created it.

3. *We must recognize the Bible to be a human document.* What we have been saying points inescapably to a conclusion. The Bible is a *human* book. Now, I am not saying that it is nothing *more* than a human book, or that its religious value and authority is no more for Christians than other books of devotion or religion. Nor am I saying that it is not the unique and decisive book of divine revelation. But I am urging that we cannot understand its divine character until we accept the very real human element through which God has chosen to speak. Our proper concern for the dignity and authority of Scripture has sometimes led us into a position regarding Scripture which is not only not true to the facts, but comes close to a kind of biblical docetism.

Docetism was an early doctrine or understanding of Christ which so emphasized Christ's deity that it denied his true humanity and so denied the incarnation. It felt that to admit that Christ was truly human was to corrupt his purity and lessen his authority. Thus he was said to be a divine figure, a "theophany" which didn't really become flesh, hunger, suffer or die, but only seemed (*doceo*, "to seem") or pretended to do so. But the church wisely saw that in the interest of Christ's authority the docetists had deprived man of a Savior who was really like man and therefore could be his high priest and representative. They also saw that such a view made nonsense of the obvious humanity of Jesus in the New Testament, as manifested, for example, in the wilderness temptation, in Gethsemane, and on the cross. Therefore docetism was rejected by the church as a heresy, although it still persists in much popular Christology.

Now, much thought about the Scriptures borders on a kind of biblical docetism because with the good intention of preserving its dignity and authority it strips the Bible of the human dimension which is so necessarily a part of its witness and so obviously a fact. By denying the real human element of Scripture we do it no service, and we deny what each of us knows from his own Christian experience, namely, that God always works through human agency. Thus to paraphrase Paul Tillich, when one asks of us, "Do you think the Bible is merely a human book?" we need to learn to answer, "Not less than a human book! Tho' for those who answer to the name of Christian, it is immeasurably more!"

What do we mean, "inspired"?

The description of the Bible as a growing, human creation of the worshiping community raises a series of important questions, most of which are related to a doctrine commonly held by Christians and more or less formally sanctioned by most historical communions. This is the doctrine of inspiration. Christians are accustomed to speaking of the Bible as divinely inspired, and when they do so they are trying to say that it has final authority or at least special authority for faith. But if the Scripture is human, what does it mean to say it is "inspired"?

To begin with we need to remind ourselves that the concept of inspiration is only marginally a biblical concept. This of course does not disqualify it, for the church has learned to use many nonbiblical terms to clarify the meaning of its faith. It does, however, require that we examine its meaning and ask how it came to be used by the church. The English word *inspiration* translates the Greek *theopneustos* meaning "God-breathed." Our word *inspire* and its several cognates carry the same suggestion. One who inspires breathes in. One who expires breathes out, for the last time, presumably. The basic idea then in inspiration is that God has breathed through or in the Scripture. In both Hebrew and Greek, the idea of breath was closely associated with that of life. Thus *pneuma*, "breath," is also the word used for spirit, the vivifying part of the body, without which it would be only a corpse. Inspiration was therefore originally a "living" idea, suggesting that the presence of God as Spirit in Scripture gave these writings a living vitality.

Accordingly, whatever meaning we give to inspiration must preserve this understanding. The Scriptures are inspired insofar as God lives and breathes within them and through them. On the other hand, the word becomes of doubtful value when it loses this living character and is intended to suggest some "quality" which the books possess quite apart from their power to communicate the living presence of God. And it is cheapened almost beyond recall when inspiration becomes a kind of special ingredient in the Bible which other books don't possess, something equivalent to "Ingredient X" or "Fluoristan" which gives our book the edge over others. Such a view puts us in the unenviable position of having to defend the existence of this "Ingredient X" without very good evidences. Usually we fall back on some theory of infallibility and this leads us into a meaningless series of "games," by which we seek to "prove" inspiration by appeal to fulfilled prophecies, miracles or the like. But the usual result is that *no one is convinced by these arguments except those who already believe.*

It is a significant fact that there was almost no interest in a doctrine of inspiration in the Apostolic church. This is because when one is aware of the power of the Spirit he doesn't worry about the authority of the Word. The living presence of God in church and Scripture argued for itself. The idea of inspiration appears to have grown up in the church for two reasons, one healthy and one less so:

1. *It arose as an "explanatory" doctrine.* That is, it was the church's attempt to express and explain the living power of these writings which spoke to them the Word of God and called them to repentance. Notice then that they did not hang the authority of the Scripture on the doctrine of inspiration, as is so often the case today. The argument was not thus, "The Scriptures are inspired; therefore they must have authority for us and we must believe them," but rather, "The Scriptures have authority for us because they speak to us the truth of God! We cannot deny them! They must be inspired!" The order is critical. Inspiration is not the starting point of the Bible's authority. It is a conclusion based on and drawn from that authority. This is the healthy source of the idea of inspiration.

2. *It became a defensive doctrine.* In the centuries following the apostolic age the immediate sense of the power of God in the church began to cool for many reasons. Other interpretations of Christ began to arise to challenge the mainline doctrine of the emerging church. How does one answer or refute such critics? One answer was to develop a "polemic" doctrine of inspiration, the purpose of which was to stop the mouth of dissenters by appeal to an infallible book of doctrine. But whenever it becomes necessary to bulwark the Bible by such a rigid concept of inspiration, we are confessing that the actual power of the Scriptures has

subsided and that it cannot convince by its own impact. And
when this has become the case, it is doubtful that any efforts
of ours to shore it up by inspiration will suffice.

Thus inspiration must remain always an explanatory doctrine, and refer to the fact that God *speaks to us* in living
power through this book. It is a way of saying that we confront God in his Spirit in its pages. This means, of course,
that we cannot really talk of "God's speaking" if we do not
also talk of our hearing and responding. We speak of the
Bible as the Word of God, but Word, like inspiration, is a
living concept. And there is no Word, no speaking unless
there is also hearing.

I am sometimes asked if the Bible is the Word of God for
a person if he does not hear, if it does not move him to
repentance. Now I suppose there is a manner of speaking in
which one can answer, "Yes, it is still the Word of God,"
but I confess that I cannot see what religious value there is
to say so, if it does not communicate to someone his word of
acceptance and love. For the Word of God to be the Word
of God *for me*, there must be appropriation. This is why the
church has usually spoken not only of inspiration but also of
illumination. When God speaks (what we might call "giving
grace") he also quickens the heart to hear by the Spirit
("receiving grace"). In the final analysis then, the Bible is
inspired if it "speaks" to you. If it does not, then its inspiration is an academic matter at best.

What I have said raises another question. Is it proper to
call the Bible the "Word of God"? Again, there is a certain
sense in which it is correct to speak of it so, as I have done
above. But there is a need for caution at this point, because
the expression "Word of God" has a more specific and also
a wider meaning than the Bible. In the broadest sense, any
speaking of God to us (through preaching, through doctrine,
or directly to the heart of the believer) can be called the
Word of God. Thus we must not be so arbitrary as to demand
of God that he *never* speak anywhere except in Scripture,

even though our experience is that he does most frequently speak through this medium. So the Word of God can be understood in a wider sense than Scripture. But it also has a narrower meaning than Scripture. Indeed, the expression "the Word of God," *ho logos tou theou,* in the New Testament normally refers not to the Bible at all but to the one who is himself the ultimate revelation and living "Word" of God. "In the beginning was the Word . . . and the Word was God . . . and the Word became flesh and dwelt among us." The Bible can be called God's Word insofar as it bears witness to him who *was* God's Word, God's self-communication, and we must not let ourselves forget this primacy of Jesus Christ himself.

I am afraid that in many evangelical circles the Word of God has come to mean exclusively the Bible, and if this is so we are in danger of making an idol of the Scriptures themselves. A few years ago I was directing a choir in the singing of the hymn "Break Thou the Bread of Life." I asked the choir what the phrase "bread of life" meant, and a member answered, "The nourishing Word of God." So far so good! So I asked, "What is this Word of God the song speaks of?" She answered, "Why, the Bible, of course." So I read the words of the hymn with proper emphasis, and she could make nothing of them:

> *Beyond* the sacred *page,* I seek *thee,* Lord!
> My spirit pants for *thee,* O *living* Word.

Two questions remain to be answered, one briefly, the other demanding a more thorough answer:

Is the Bible Theology?

Insofar as the Bible contains the reflection of believers and of the church on its faith it contains theology, and in some degree is theology. Since the theology it contains is that of those who knew the Savior and his redemptive work firsthand

and participated in the birth of the community of faith, it remains a uniquely rich and irreplaceable source for our theology. But not even the theology of the Apostolic church can be allowed to take the place of a personal theology.

Are We Bound by the Bible?

We have said that one's own theology is born out of dialogue, and that three members of the dialogue, Bible, church and believer, are central. Therefore to the question, "Are we bound by the authority of the Bible?" we must give a two-fold reply. We must first answer yes. If our theology is to be Christian theology, it cannot escape the Bible. There are at least four reasons why this is so:

(1) It is the only source of information concerning Jesus Christ, who is the focal point of every properly Christian theology. (2) It is the original witness and confession to Christ. We can never come nearer, historically speaking, to the redemptive event than we do in the Apostolic church. The persistent desire of the church to return to the New Testament and to the faith of the Apostolic church is an expression of this conviction. (3) It has continued to create the church. While it is true that the church created the Scriptures, it is equally true that the church through the centuries has found a power for correction and for renewal in the Scriptures. Scripture re-creates church! The church has returned again and again to the prophets and apostles for its own dynamic and life. (4) It has forced itself upon us! In the final analysis, the only answer the church can give to the question, "Why this book and not another?" is Karl Barth's answer. We haven't had a choice! Other books have been helpful, but this one has *seized* us, required us to hear, and refused to let us go! It has been "inspired," breathed with the power and word of God. Finally no other answer than this can be given to the question, "Why the Bible?"

And the church can scarcely anticipate a time when it will be otherwise. We are bound to its word. We cannot do theology without it.

But to the question, "Are we bound by the Bible?" we must also answer no, for within the dialogue of faith are other sources of insight which we must hear. Our theology is not exclusively biblical theology, even if we formally hold to an exclusive biblical authority, because we continually measure, test and select from biblical insights in the light of the belief of the church and in the light of our own experience. Now once again, I am not saying that we *should*, but that we *do*. We are continually selecting from the vast reservoir of religion which is the Bible those passages which are most able to express our understanding of faith. The process of selection is often subtle, so that we may not even notice that in returning frequently to a few passages we exclude others, but the selectivity is no less real. Ministers habitually preach from texts which speak to them and just as habitually avoid other passages, because for various reasons these passages do not say what they wish to say. What pastor preaches on Obadiah with his little "hymn of hate" to Edom as often as he does the thirteenth chapter of 1 Corinthians? And is this not so because the history of the church and the experience of the Christian heart see love as the center of faith and feel uncomfortable with hate? To select is to exercise judgment in the name of some critical principle which itself is not properly scriptural.

But not only do we select, we interpret! And every interpretation of the Bible is in some sense an attempt to explain difficult and unclear passages on the basis of some more certain principle, usually theological. In my own tradition it is often asserted that we do not interpret the Bible by tradition or by personal standards but by the Bible itself. Scripture interprets Scripture. This is a Reformation principle but it is far older than Luther. What this means, though, is that we interpret the uncertain and unclear passages by the clear and explicit ones. But what determines which passages are clear and decisive? Usually our tradition.

For example, on the surface there appears to be a real theological tension between the doctrine of salvation expressed in Ephesians and in James. Paul says, "By grace are ye saved through faith . . . not of works, lest any man should boast." James says, "Faith without works is dead." Interpreters in the Baptist fellowship always opt for Paul, explaining that James really isn't saying what he appears to say, namely, that one's works are a factor in his salvation. But James really seems rather explicit. How can we say he means something else? Why, because the New Testament clearly rejects works salvation! But is this really so? There are numerous passages, including the words of Jesus himself, which could be understood to teach works righteousness. Why not say these are the clear teachings of the New Testament? Isn't the real reason the fact that we are in the tradition of the Reformers whose fundamental principle of justification by faith alone has determined our own understanding of salvation? Thus we choose Paul not because his meaning is clearly the meaning of the New Testament but because his understanding agrees with *our* understanding, and we reject James (or reinterpret him) because he seems to stand in another tradition.

We may also interpret, translate, evaluate the Bible in the light of our Christian conscience. Thus we may reject a seemingly clear intention because it seems unworthy of God or of one of his people. Thus when the Book of Exodus or Paul speaks of God hardening Pharaoh's heart, we may reject this by saying that what they mean is that Pharaoh hardened his own heart. Or when Jesus curses a fig tree, apparently, according to the text, because he was hungry and it had no fruit, we hasten to say that wasn't the *real* reason, and explain that the withering was an acted parable of Israel's rejection. Why so? It nowhere says this. But surely, it must be so, because Jesus wasn't the kind who went around spitefully withering trees! Agreed! But isn't it our conviction of what Christ was like born out of Bible and tradition and personal experience of his love which leads us to reject what *appears* to be unworthy of him?

I have labored this point because it may be a critical one for those in the most strongly biblical tradition. For such a person it will be easy to see and admit that we qualify the other members of the dialogue by Scripture, but not so easy to see that every attempt to evaluate or to interpret represents a qualification of the scriptural witness. No Christian, no matter how literalistic he claims to be, can avoid doing this. And we must understand that *in so doing we do not weaken the witness of our theology but strengthen it*. We are right to determine what Scripture can mean in the light of faith. We are right to call the withered fig tree an "acted parable," because this makes sense in the light of what we have come to know of Christ in Scripture, in the church, and in our personal forgiveness.

Thus we are bound to Scripture as one of the indispensable members of the dialogue of faith, but it is also a part of the larger dialogue, which includes both church and personal experience. We must now look at the contribution of the church to the continuing dialogue.

SUGGESTIONS FOR THOUGHT
AND DISCUSSION

1. How does the Bible function in your fellowship or church? How much authority does it have? How is the Bible used? In your opinion, is its authority growing or declining?

2. What role does the Bible play in your personal life? Is its influence greater now than in the past?

3. Write down as many affirmations or statements about the Bible as you can. Organize these into a systematic "The-

ology of the Scriptures." Are there ideas included that conflict or are in tension? How can they be brought into agreement?

4. What evidences can you point to in the Bible which
seem to reinforce or confirm the following ideas?

   a. That there is a human element in the Scriptures.
   b. That the Bible reflects a "world view" or "cosmology"
      different from our own.
   c. That the Bible contains a diversity of beliefs and atti-
      tudes.
   d. That the Bible is "divine," "inspired" or of God.

5. Respond to the following questions (or, if practical,
have a friendly debate between two individuals or groups):

   a. "If you can't trust the Bible on everything, you can't
      trust it on anything."
   b. "The Bible is God's Word whether we believe it or not."
   c. "Every word in the Bible is literally true."

CHAPTER FIVE

The Community of Faith

WE HAVE ARGUED THAT OUR THEOLOGY must draw from and be regulated by the Word of God as present in the Scripture. Thus Scripture becomes a basic source-norm for faith. But out of the Christ-event has come a community of faith, a historical reality which is traditionally called the church, and every Christian has his roots deep within this community. Thus our ways of thinking and our ways of theologizing have been profoundly shaped by our participation in this community. We need now to look briefly at the way in which the worshiping community, past and present, enters into a personal theology.

Are We Bound by the Church?

Again we must answer yes and no; no, in the sense that the community and its word of faith must constantly be judged by Scripture and experience. If the church as a historical institution becomes the sole authority for faith or if its tradition is exempt from criticism, we are likely to develop the kind of ecclesiastical absolutism which marked the late Middle Ages and which smothers creative personal faith. More will be said of this danger in our discussion of anti-creedalism. Thus the Christian must be prepared to be a nay-sayer to the church. But we must also answer yes, in that we can no more escape the church or ignore what it has said than we can ignore or escape the Scripture.

Now, if we are speaking of the church as a present fact, many will recognize a commitment to it and the necessity of hearing its word concerning faith. But are we bound to the past? The answer again must be yes, although the faulty sense of history common to Americans and reinforced, in my own communion at least, by a tradition of separatism from established churches often obscures this dependence. The historic community of faith serves as a major source of doctrine and as a deep and rich stream from which we may draw our personal theology. It also serves as a norm against which we must constantly check our doctrine. To every new insight we must continually bring the measure of the past, asking the question, "What have Christians of the past had to say concerning this matter?"

The church cannot be ignored because out of it has come our own Christian faith. Again, we of a nonhistorical tradition often have an almost totally negative view of the church. The Anabaptists of the sixteenth century viewed the whole of Christian history as a betrayal of the gospel and themselves as the first true church since Constantine. There was for them no history of doctrine but only a history of heresy. Luther saw more wisely that for all of its corruption and error, the church had carried enough of the grace and truth of God to cause *him* to become a Christian. Thus while he could attack its error and shame it for its corruption, he could not repudiate it. Had it not given him life? "The church is my mother," he wrote. He then added significantly, "A whore she surely is! But she is my mother." For all of her fallibility and error, the community of the past remains

the womb which has borne us, the breasts which have nourished us, and a profound and often unconscious source of
our faith and doctrine. And since faith creates community,
it is inconceivable that Christian faith and theology are
possible without *some* form of church. A churchless Christianity is finally unthinkable. We are bound by the community of faith.

But What Community?

The church in history has been many churches and the
church of the present is often divided into mutually exclusive
sects. Yet in the plethora of churches and denominations
there are roots of commonness, sometimes theological, sometimes merely historical, which bind groups together and determine the specific form of the church which has given us
life. These common roots will characteristically shape our
personal theology. Thus each person's theology, however it
may develop, will reflect the qualities of faith and understanding which distinguish his native group. In other words,
my theology will always be "Baptist" theology, and even
more decisively, the theology of those particular local
churches where I have been born and nourished in the faith.
And since most specific Christian fellowships belong historically to larger "families" in which the forms and thought-life
are similar, the historical community of faith for each of us
can be described in a series of concentric circles. This concentric pattern suggests both the value of the smallest communion to the believer who is a part of it and the unity of
that smallest element with the "church" in its most universal
historical sense. And each of these "communities" of faith
has a bearing on the "shape" which my personal theology
takes. They all structure the way I think even about Scripture
and about my own experience of grace. I tend to interpret
Scripture in the light of the church, and I tend to concep-
tualize my own religious experience (my conversion experi-

ence, for example) along the lines my fellowship understands
to be normative.

So if I answer the question, "What community?" it must
be by a series of answers of increasingly larger scope. I will
use my own answer to this question to illustrate what I
mean, and the reader can make his own appropriate substitu-
tion. What community indeed?

1. *The Baptist community.* I am a part of a particular
fellowship which has, no doubt, shaped my fundamental
ways of feeling and thinking my faith. My commitment to
this community is, I hope, not a slavish or exclusive one, but
it is a commitment nevertheless, and what it lacks in universality it makes up for in concreteness and immediacy.
This is where the real life of the church exists, where the joy
and agony of worship, mission and fellowship happen. For
this very reason, one is apt to see the least ideal, most profoundly human side of the community of faith here, and
for this reason, among others, it is easy to belittle its values
and even to doubt its usefulness to the sophisticated believer.
The attitude of many believers who are irked by the pettiness
and fallibility of the local, or institutional, church is reminiscent of the humanist who confesses that he loves *humanity*
but can't stand people. It is easy to love an ideal abstraction
called church and to be offended and alienated by the concrete humanity of the tangible community. But only a theology which is hammered out in the heat of concrete involvement in a concrete community is apt to have the pragmatic
ruggedness to survive in a real world.

2. *The Protestant community.* As a Baptist, I am also a
member of a larger community of faith which I call, in its
usual sense, the Protestant community. Within this broad
variety of Christian faith I include, as we have commonly
come to do, those groups which descend theologically from
the classical reformers, Luther, Calvin and Zwingli, but also
that broad strain of similar Christianity called Sectarian or
Anabaptist. Though there are technical distinctions, the kind

of faith they represent is so similar at heart that they have become interwoven like a great tapestry in European and American history. My own denomination has its roots deep in the Anabaptist tradition; but it has also drawn deeply from Calvin and Zwingli, and to a lesser degree from Luther, so that in my college and seminary days I frequently studied from textbooks written, for example, by Presbyterians. Is it any wonder then that Baptists, Presbyterians and Methodists —all of whom share this same tradition—should find so few real barriers between them? And my sense of being a part of this larger community will also infuse my theology. My theology will still be Baptist, but it will also be Protestant theology.

There are, of course, other fellowships. The man who is a product of a different community—let us say, the Roman Catholic—will find his theology infused by different forms and expressions. And this is as it should be. Insofar as the differences in the historical community are not permitted to erect impenetrable walls between Christians, they can contribute to the enrichment of the common faith we hold.

3. *The Christian community.* The ultimate circle of faith must be that which is able to encompass all the lesser circles, namely the historic Christian community in its broadest sense. Insofar as each smaller fellowship considers itself to be committed to Christ as the focal point of God's redemptive work and to be descended from the historical community which arose from his work, then it is included in a common fellowship with all other such communities. Thus, while we must not lose the concreteness of the smallest circle of faith, we must learn to appreciate the degree to which we are in debt to the church at large and must recognize that an adequate personal theology has to reflect this greater universality of perspective. Only a sense of being bound to the Christian community and of participating in its oneness can enable us to avoid becoming sects and falling victim to the spirit of Pharisaism.

How Does the Experience of
the Community Come to Us?

How can a believer get access to the riches of the past in order that they might become source and norm for his personal theology? A full answer would be exceedingly complex, since the life of the church is complex, but some of the more obvious sources can be mentioned:

1. *Again, the Bible.* Here is the record of a particular and critical manifestation of the church, the apostolic community.

2. *The creeds and confessions of the church and churches.* The first Christian creeds probably grew out of the early baptismal formulas which were, in the strictest sense, public confessions of faith preliminary to receiving baptism. Thus the original intent was to express in the briefest possible words the essence of the *kerygma* and of faith. Since this irreducible essence was the theological basis of the church— and creeds are theology—these creeds became the test of whether one shared the same faith and hope, and therefore they became tests of fellowship. Now it is a fact that they were frequently elevated from confession to dogma and made the sole acceptable source and norm of theology, therefore destroying the dialogue of faith by denying other communities or individuals any word of correction. This is the danger that creeds always present. They can become crystallized and freeze the dialogue of faith.

But this danger should not blind us to the valuable functions which creeds have served and continue to serve in the life of the church. Nor should it close our eyes to the value of the various Christian confessions as reservoirs for Christian faith and theology. A creed gives the community shape by helping it to see clearly what is its common faith so that it can give assent to that faith. As a result the identity and purpose of the community are reinforced. The function of the creed was infinitely important during the Middle Ages when the vast majority of believers were illiterate and unable to grasp even the rudiments of the great classical Christian past. But they could learn by heart and pass on to their children the essence of the gospel, thus keeping their faith alive by means of the Apostles' Creed or a similar confession. It is scarcely too much to say that through ten centuries of Latin liturgy and illiteracy the creed, in its many forms and manifestations (in hymns and carols, in the symbolism of the church year, etc.), was the life of faith for the masses.

Those of us in the free church traditions have tended to be suspicious of creeds, seeing them not only as authoritarian and oppressive but as unnecessary substitutes for a sense of God in the heart. These they may be, and they may also become crutches for weak faith. But who is to say if we can do entirely without creeds? My own fellowship is as anti-creedal as any, yet we have "confessions of faith" which serve largely the same functions, and which tend to develop the same authoritative status. Indeed, because such authority is informal it is often unconscious and therefore all the more powerful. And since we are without formal creeds in the proper sense we are given to employing various kinds of "church covenants" of uncertain origin and doubtful theological value, which are really crypto-creeds. The persistence of such informal creeds points to the need of some kind of summary of faith for most Christians.

At any rate, one can do well in his search for a personal theology to inquire into what the church has said in its great confessions of past and present. He should never approach them uncritically, but should view them for what they are: the witness of the Christian community to the meaning of its corporate faith. They are not infallible, but their insights are often so true and their expression so trenchant and seemingly timeless that it is difficult not to marvel, especially when one considers the extremely human circumstances of their creation. For example, the great Nicene-Constantinopolitan Creed which gave classic expression to the doctrine of God and the Creed of Chalcedon which defined the orthodox doctrine of Christ were hammered out in the most unsavory series of political sessions, as my professor Langdon Gilkey would say, "complete with hoods and smoke-filled rooms." Yet you and I would be hard-put to formulate a summary of faith which is in the same ball park with these. It is no wonder that the church has seen in them the guiding presence of God's Spirit.

What I have said above should not be taken as a rejection of anticreedalism in principle, but a suggestion that it must be applied with intelligence and understanding. I share with my Anabaptist forebears a distrust of the creedal mentality, but I also recognize that anticreedalism can be self-deceptive. We may attack the creedalism of others and obscure the fact that we have our own working creeds, official or not. We may also by our anticreedal stance obscure our own need for a word from the past and our dependence on the historic church. We may become theological iconoclasts.

The virtues of creedalism and anticreedalism may be understood in terms of the dialogue of faith which we have described. The chief virtue of anticreedalism is that it guards the other members of the dialogue from the tyranny of the past, that is, from the temptation of the church with its traditions and its creeds to demand exclusive attention and loyalty, and therefore to smother the individual in his attempt to give expression to his faith. Anticreedalism keeps the dialogue alive and prevents the absolutizing of tradition. It says, "As important as the church is as a source of faith, it is not the only source, and it is not infallible. It must be continually examined, modified, and affirmed by the experience of the believer." Creeds tend to "freeze" theology. Anticreedalism thaws it out. The anticreedal instinct preserves mainly the third member of the dialogue; it keeps theology *ours*. Creedalism, on the other hand, reminds us that we cannot do theology without the past, and reminds us of the bond of unity between us and the church of the past. Creedalism keeps theology unified, concrete and anchored to history; it keeps it *Christian*.

3. *The theology of past and present.* While the church's confessions present the heart of Christian faith in theological form they are by no means the total heritage of its faith. And one cannot begin to develop a rich personal faith without some contact with the great theological expressions of the past. Now much of this we have absorbed indirectly through its influence on preaching, Christian devotional literature, and culture in general. Nevertheless, the lay theologian would do well to expose himself to some of the great hearts and spirits which Christian faith has created in past and present. Such an acquaintance may have to begin as a matter of discipline, but he may find his taste for theological reading growing as he discovers his kinship with those he reads and finds his own faith illuminated and challenged. Many classics of Christian faith and devotion are accessible to the lay reader and can help to make him aware of his heritage. The bibliography at the end of this book is a starting point for such study.

4. *The church at worship and at work.* Up until now we have been speaking largely of the church as a past reality, but it is a source and norm of faith also in its contemporary existence. The Christian who is tempted to develop a theological idea not only asks himself, "What say the creeds?" or "What say the past centuries of faith?" but also, "How will this go with my brethren? What will they say when they hear it? Will they confirm it? Can it be confirmed by the church at worship and at work?" This is the reason why theology must always be "church" theology, even for those who by their personal experience are led to call in question the institution which gives it expression in their day.

The believer cannot develop a theology in isolation from the church. The prophet who challenged and judged the community of Israel drew his spiritual strength and his identity from it. And the person who has no contemporary relation to the worshiping community, whatever form it may take, has a doubtful relation to the church of the past. Thus one develops a personal theology in the midst of the life of the community. And his theology will reflect the influence of that community of forgiveness, both in its negative aspects—its human limitation, its imperfections, its failure—and in its positive expressions of faith, hope and love. It is no accident that the creeds grew out of an act of worship, namely, baptism, and any adequate personal theology must draw deeply from the life of fellowship in the community of which the believer is a part.

SUGGESTIONS FOR THOUGHT
AND DISCUSSION

1. What is the attitude of your church or denomination to other churches? Does it stress its similarity to others or its distinctness?

2. To what other faiths or fellowships do you feel the closest relationships? Why? Are the reasons theological or cultural? (Do they arise from similar religious ideas or from a similar way of life?)

3. What do you know about the "family tree" of your church? Have a "scholarly" member of the group do some research on the subject.

4. Does your church or denomination have a formal creed or confession of faith? Study it carefully and answer the following questions:

   a. How much of it are you able to understand clearly?
   b. How much of it do you believe?
   c. How much of it do you really respond to?

(If the group is of mixed denominational background, a comparison of creeds and statements of faith might be instructive. How much common ground exists? What are the points of difference?)

CHAPTER SIX

You!

THE THIRD MEMBER OF THE DIALOGUE of faith, and therefore the third source-norm for a personal theology, is the believer himself as he lives his life with the Spirit of God, with the believing community, and with the world. Everything which presents itself, whether from the Scriptures or from the church past and present, claiming, "This is Christian theology," must be evaluated by the believer. He must ask himself whether in the light of his experience of redemption such theology can be affirmed and can be allowed to speak for him as his own. Thus I, as a Christian, must continually draw from my own Christian experience the raw materials of theology, and use them to judge both church and Scripture.

But do I have the right to judge church and Scripture? If I allow my own judgment to determine what I will accept and what I will reject from creed or Bible, then do I not fall into the most dangerous of traps, that of subjectivism? Are not rigid biblicism and traditionalism to be preferred in the end to subjectivism? The question is not to be dismissed lightly, for the charge of subjectivism in theology has historical justification. Are we free to say what we will or to write theology as we want it to be? If in fact we are sinners and not inclined to hear the harsh word of judgment, will we not always cut theology to the pattern of our selfish desires? We must answer that this is a very real risk, but we cannot escape the risk of subjectivism by a retreat into objectivism; we cannot escape from the tension of being a Christian in the world by a narrow biblicism or "churchism," both of which place all the sources and norms for faith outside of the believer.

Subjectivism runs the risk of selfish distortion, but objectivism runs the risk of becoming a matter of the past, and irrelevant to the crises of the believer's life and world. Since my faith is *my* faith, it must bear the stamp of my experience and be wrought out in the crucible of my life. If this is subjectivism, then it must be called a "good" subjectivism, not only because it is inescapable, but because it alone can keep the faith of the individual and of the church in living contact with the world. We should also be reminded that this member of the dialogue of faith, the self, stands always under the norms of church and Scripture, the "objective" poles of theology. It therefore cannot properly be allowed to slip into an open-ended subjectivism which would make every theologian a law unto himself. My subjectivity is regulated by the subjectivity of the church present and past.

The "Internal" Dialogue

Precisely because my experience is the subjective experience of a living person, this source and norm of faith is apt to appear more complex and less clearly definable than the others, and as consisting of different elements of the self in tension or struggle with one another. In other words, while the dialogue of faith is a dialogue of the believer with the sources and norms of faith *outside* of himself, there is also an "internal" dialogue within the Christian who strives to unify his whole life under God. And each element of his experience, each circle in which he lives, learns, and acts will become a source of theology for him. We may suggest three closely related and overlapping aspects of personal experience which must play a part in determining the content of the believer's theology:

1. *His specifically Christian experience.* Strangely enough, those who insist that theology should keep up-to-date by opening itself up to all aspects of modern experience frequently overlook or ignore the fundamental aspect of that experience which makes it Christian. I cannot be a Christian theologian unless there is a sense of participation in God through Jesus Christ, however that participation be described. As Paul Tillich has rightly pointed out, the specific character of our Christian experience will vary for reasons both sociological and psychological, so that we must be careful in setting standards to which all must conform. As our needs or our understanding of our needs vary, so will our way of conceiving our experience of God. One whose need expresses itself in guilt and alienation may grasp God as forgiveness. One who is fragmented and directionless may speak of healing. But insofar as the reality which the church has called redemption through Christ is a part of his experience, then everything else he experiences becomes a part of that redeemed life and will be understood in its light. It is through the life of the Spirit which dwells within each believer that we become theologians.

2. *His experience as a person.* Since all of life stands in relation to one's life as a believer, then every experience which enriches his life as a person is drawn into his life as a Christian. His faith must reflect his sense of need, fellowship, pain, community, love, frustration, his encounters with friends, engagements with enemies, birth, death—all of these become the raw materials of faith, and the Christian must be prepared to ask of each new experience, "What new questions does this experience raise concerning life, faith and God? And what new answers does it suggest or provide?"

3. *His experience as a modern person.* There has always

been a "modern world," and faith has always been called upon to face that world and to make the journey of risk, to wrestle with the new challenges which ever confront it. But it is no exaggeration to say that the Christian faith today faces a more critical or more demanding task than at any time in its history. Not even the cultural crisis of the sixth century that saw Rome fall and the great Western culture emerge from Rome's collapse can compare as a time of crisis for faith. Indeed, we are now confronted by a world so radically new in its perspectives and so swift in its change that many have concluded that Christianity and even religion have become relics of the past with no word to speak to this world. Today's Christian must hear the many words of challenge, must discern the questions and the accusations they contain and must wrestle with them if the gospel is to be a word of grace for future as well as past. There is no dimension of modern experience that can be overlooked and no question which can be evaded. We must ask about Belsen and Buchenwald, Vietnam and the impotence of the church, about computers and quasars, about Marshall McLuhan and cryobionics. And we must ask about them and struggle with them, not just because modern men are demanding answers, but because *we*, as modern men, are asking about them and wanting answers. It is as modern men that we as Christians must forge a faith and a theology. Else we will not only lose a hearing from those without, but we will find our own confidence eroded by the growing acids of unresolved and un-dealt-with experience.

The demands made on faith by the modern world help to further underscore the need for lay theologians, because no man, trained theologian or otherwise, can know all of the areas of modern life with sufficient depth to speak about them effectively. The professional theologian must seek to be knowledgeable in many areas. He must read drama, poetry and literature; he must know in general what is happening in biology, physics, astronomy; he must have an acquaintance with sociology and psychology. But he can in most of these be only an interested outsider, a theologian who *reads* science and tries not to invalidate his theology by the obvious faux pas. What we need are scientist-theologians, sociologist-theologians, literary theologians, medical and biological theologians, industrial and commercial theologians—laymen in every area who precisely because they are experts in their particular fields and because they are Christians can contribute with special force and clarity to that aspect of modern existence.

Asking the Questions of Faith

In summary, then, theology emerges from a living encounter of the believer with God through past and present. Thus, when confronted by the challenge of life, how do we in principle move toward an answer to the questions raised by its challenge? We might schematize the dialogue of faith by the following steps. The believer asks of each confrontation:

1. *What is its religious meaning?* That is, what is the real question at stake here? What, behind the complexity of the situation, is the real issue confronting faith?
2. What does the Scripture say?
3. What does the church, past and present, say?
4. What does my life and experience demand?

Two Theological Yardsticks for Your Theology

On the basis of what has been said before, we can conclude this first part of our study by suggesting two standards against which the lay theologian should be able to measure the adequacy of any theological formulation. Now, these are formal guides only. They do not have to do with the actual content of doctrine but only with determining what *in principle* could be called an adequate expression of faith. These "tests" or yardsticks are basically those suggested by Friedrich Schleiermacher, the nineteenth century theologian who more than any other charted the way which theology has taken since his day. We will, however, modify his terminology and extend somewhat the meaning of his second standard:

1. *Religious validity.* Schleiermacher called this yardstick "ecclesiastical validity." By this he meant that a theological proposition is valid and useful if it accurately expresses the religious experience of the church or the individual employing it. If it does so, the believer is apt to "recognize" himself and his experience in it and answer, "Yes, this says it! This is what it is all about!" Now, once again, no theological proposition ever expresses fully the reality of faith, but a person can formulate his experience more or less well, and the theological statement which comes closest to reflecting the reality of faith is apt to be most satisfying to the believer, and is also more apt to create response and to survive in the life of the community.

Every Christian has heard a sermon or read a theological description of Christian faith and has had the uncomfortable sensation that it just didn't ring true. Although it made *some* contact with Christian experience, it finally distorted more than it expressed. Such a description, for such a listener at least, lacks religious validity. For example, I find myself responding in such a way to descriptions of God which in an effort to avoid the difficulties inherent in traditional theism deny to him the decisive qualities of personhood. While I understand what those who use such nonpersonal language are seeking to do, I know that there is something fundamentally wrong-headed in the result. The God they speak of simply doesn't fit the reality of grace and forgiveness which I have experienced in the church. I reject such an impersonal view of God because it is out of harmony with the character of God revealed in the church's confession and in my own experience of grace.

Every theology must continually be compared with these basic experiences of salvation, worship, and devotion to see if it is giving a truthful description of them; and the theologian should constantly strive to bring his statement of faith and his experience of faith into ever closer conformity. Thus I must continually ask myself of my personal theology, "Does it accurately reflect the reality of faith?"

2. *Fruitfulness.* Theology must not only be religiously valid, it must also be fruitful. Now Schleiermacher meant by fruitfulness the ability of a doctrinal statement or idea to lead one effectively into an examination and understanding of the rest of faith and life. A doctrine is fruitful if it opens up one's theology. I am sometimes asked where one ought to start the study of theology. There is no single starting place. For certain practical reasons, it may be preferable to begin with God, or revelation, or some other specific doctrine, but these are matters of convenience. Since faith seeks to deal with all of life and to unify it under the grace of God, then theology must have both comprehensiveness and unity. A person can literally begin anywhere that God and life confront him; but wherever he starts, he should find himself led naturally to ask about all the other elements of life under God. If he begins with man asking, "What is this strange creature who dies like a dog, but unlike the dog knows that he dies?" he is led to ask not only about man but also about creation, about meaning, about forgiveness, about hope, about God. If he asks about God first, then he must ask what it is to be man before him. Is God good? Why then is there evil? And so on.

Some types of theology stifle this kind of fruitfulness. A badly stated doctrine of God may make it impossible to talk meaningfully about redemption or to make sense out of the Christian understanding of man—for example, if we deny to God any capacity for human sympathy (as the traditional doctrine of God's "impassability" seems to do) or identify him with impersonal energy. So we must ask at every point,

"If I express my faith in these terms will it open up new areas for growth and shed new light on the rest of faith or will it inhibit further development?" Thus while one kind of theological formulation may not be essentially wrong, yet another may be preferable because of its greater potential for fruitfulness.

Such a possibility of being led "from faith to faith" within one's theology implies that there is to be expected a kind of inner consistency to it. This does not mean that we are able to solve the mysteries of life and faith and make God an open book. It is one aspect of the essence of God that he continually transcends us, and it is the character of theology that in its human limitation it never exhausts its object, God. But the principle of consistency means that we must be exceedingly careful not to avoid difficulties in our theology by pleading the mystery of God. Nor should we refuse to accept the responsibility for bad or contradictory theology by piously appealing to faith. It is this habit of fleeing from our own inconsistencies and shabby thinking or hiding behind a smoke screen of humble faith (while, incidentally, allowing no such retreat to our theological opponents) which has led to the frequent charges of dishonesty and hypocrisy directed toward the church.

Thus we can say that a theology or doctrine which opens up faith and which leads the believer into an ever deepening unity of understanding is a fruitful theology. It aims at (but never achieves) completeness coupled with fidelity to God, to self and to the world. A theology or doctrine which closes doors, which refuses to look at life or to ask honestly the questions which life raises, which encourages narrowness, rationalization, or subtle forms of dishonesty in the name of faith can be said to be unfruitful. It can also be confessed that such a theology is unworthy of Christ's church, is a form of laziness and cowardice, and a sin against the God whose name we serve.

But there is another sense in which theology should be

fruitful, and it is closely akin to the first. A theology in the last analysis justifies itself insofar as it produces Christian grace. Any theology which does not reflect the fruits of the Spirit or inhibits their growth in the believer and in the community of faith must be suspect from the beginning. If the essence of faith is that God is love, and if our theology fails to express this love in percept and action, then something is clearly out of joint. If Paul is correct that the fruits of the Spirit are love, joy, peace, patience, kindness, goodness, faithfulness, gentleness, self-control (against which, he tells us, there is no law) then these must be also the heart and the fruit of any personal theology which begins with Christ and ends by moving courageously into the world.

SUGGESTIONS FOR THOUGHT
AND DISCUSSION

1. This chapter speaks of the "internal dialogue" of faith (pp. 96–99). In what area of your experience do you feel tension between your experience as a Christian and as a modern person?

2. Are there special aspects of your life and experience which might enable you to make a real contribution to the church's theology in the modern world—for instance, areas of expertise or training, unusual experiences, special situations or roles in which you find yourself?

PART THREE

What's It All About?

(The Scope of Theology)

CHAPTER SEVEN

Surveying the Ground

IN PART I OF THIS BOOK we have been concerned with theology less as a formal academic discipline than as an activity of the Christian and of the church. We have seen that it is born out of the experience of grace, and gives expression to the life of faith as it is lived in the world. We learned that theology in this sense is no more escapable for the believer than the air about him, since he lives always within the atmosphere of his faith. Since we were concerned chiefly with the *activity* of theology, and were seeking to understand its "mechanics," so to speak, we have had little to say about its *content*. In fact, we have in most cases avoided extensive reference to traditional theological issues, such as the doctrine of God, Christology, and eschatology. This is what we had in mind when in the introduction we insisted that this book is not a book of theology. In fact, Parts I and II serve as what the Germans would call a "theological prolegomenon," that is, a fore-word which must precede the actual work of theology. It is really an essay in "theological method," intended to provide some of the tools for the job of filling in the content, and this job in the last analysis must be the reader's own.

But we have already seen that one's own personal theology never happens in a vacuum, no matter how original and creative it might be. A knowledge of the ways in which theology has been done in the past and of the traditional divisions of labor within the discipline can help the Christian understand more clearly what he is doing when he sets out to forge his own understanding of faith. Also, some inquiry into the classic expressions of Christian faith and into the persistent questions of human existence which have given rise to them can help the believer see his own efforts as a part of a continuing community activity and can provide him with invaluable material for expressing and criticizing his own theology.

Thus we can state the purpose of the remainder of the book, namely to give the reader some understanding of the scope of theology. In the present chapter we will survey the major divisions of theology, and get an overview of the development of Christian doctrine through the centuries. In subsequent chapters we will examine briefly the main concerns which have marked Christian theology from the beginning of the church's history and which have come to constitute the main divisions of Christian doctrine; for instance, the doctrines of God (theology proper), of man (anthropology), of Christ (Christology), of the church (ecclesiology), and of the Christian hope (eschatology).

Most of the critical issues of Christian theology concern aspects of one or the other of these major doctrines. As we examine each of these great areas of theological interest we will try to do briefly three things. First, we will try to understand what traditional Christian theology has had to say, especially where there has been a theological consensus of some depth among Christians. Second, we will try to discover the religious intention or insights in each of these doctrinal expressions, even when the forms of past expression may no longer be forms which we find congenial or useful. In so doing we will begin to develop and apply the theological sensitivity and taste of which we spoke in chapter two. Finally, we shall try to see the way in which the church's doctrine has taken shape in a kind of living interaction between the life of faith and the concrete historical and social situation of the church in the world. Nothing is more clear to the student of the history of doctrine than that our theology is shaped by the special needs and the particular thought patterns of its age. Thus as we understand how the theology of the past sought to answer the questions of its age in the light of faith we will be better equipped to speak with creativity to the questions which our own age puts to us.

Since this chapter and the following ones begin to look more and more like theology in the old dogmatic sense, I am prompted to renew my original caution regarding our purposes and to add a second one. First, the reader should recall that this is not a book of theology. And as we begin to deal with the content of theology, the lay theologian should be especially careful to keep his purpose in mind, namely, not just to be *told* what the content of faith should be, but to learn by example how to forge his own. In the following chapters my own theological prejudices and opinions will be reflected with increasing clarity. Still, these should provide only the grist for a personal grinding or they will not have been of much help in the development of a personal theology. Second, the following chapters make no attempt at completeness or comprehensiveness. Such an attempt would be beyond our scope and would probably work against our larger purpose. There are plenty of good books of theology, some of which are to be found in the suggested readings in the appendix. Our purpose is, by presenting glimpses here and there into the stuff of faith and by making the reader sense the way in which theology is rooted in life, to urge him to begin to wrestle with life and faith in a theological way— that is, to incite him to become a theologian.

THE AREAS OF THEOLOGY

The academic field of theology is a part of the broader field of religious or Christian studies. In most theological schools or seminaries, the curriculum of study is divided into four distinct but not entirely separate areas. The biblical area is concerned primarily with the exegesis or interpretation of the Bible and with several related disciplines, such as biblical languages and often biblical archeology. The historical area is concerned especially with the history of Christianity as a political-social reality and with the history of religion in general. The comparative study of religions is usually included in this area, although it has obvious affinities with theological studies. The theological area is concerned chiefly with the church's understanding and interpretation of its faith. The practical area is concerned with the application of the insights provided by biblical, historical and theological studies to the life of the church and the community. The practical area may include such studies as homiletics (the art of preparing and delivering sermons), church administration, psychology of religion and counseling. Sometimes Christian ethics is included in the practical area, although it is more commonly treated today as a specialized area of theological studies.

It should be clear that theology can never be done in isolation from the other areas of study we have described. For example, so long as Christian thought is truly Christian, it must remain biblical. We have already seen how the Bible remains a norm, and in some respects *the* norm, for all theology. We have also seen that theology provides the perspectives and outlooks which the biblical interpreter brings with him to the Bible. Thus the two fields complement and reinforce each other. Biblical students and theological students often carry on a good-natured rivalry which reflects the interdependence of the studies. The biblical boys assure the theological boys that without the work of the biblical interpreters the theologians would have no raw material with which to work, and the theological boys remind the biblical boys thats one "brings a theology with him to the Bible," and that his ability to interpret soundly depends on the soundness and maturity of his theology. Both have important elements of truth on their sides.

Similarly, the bond between theological and historical studies is close and gets closer every year, since the dominant approach to theology today is through a study of its historical development. The relation of practical studies to theology and to the other areas is of special importance, since the pragmatic mood of modern man makes practical application especially dear to his heart. This concern for practical application is a wholesome concern. However, it can become a temptation to ignore the less concrete but necessary work of laying a theoretical foundation as a basis for action, with resultant shallowness and shortsightedness in practical application. The effectiveness of practical Christianity is usually dependent on the soundness of the historical, theological and biblical understanding which undergirds it.

The area of theology is usually divided into at least four subdivisions. These subdivisions represent to some extent differences in the content with which they deal, but are really differences in approach, or in the way in which the content of doctrine is studied and organized. It will be worth our while to distinguish these divisions.

Biblical Theology

Biblical theology is closely related to the biblical area and is often done by those whose special training is biblical. Its purpose is to go beyond mere interpretation of particular passages and to develop the overall theological understanding of the Bible and of the particular writers and special traditions represented in the Bible. On the broadest scale it seeks

to answer such questions as, "What is the biblical understanding of God, of creation, of man, and how should such
understandings influence and shape our theology?" Biblical
theology is usually separated into Old Testament, Inter-
testamental, and New Testament theology. It seeks to describe the general theological viewpoints of each of these
major areas, and also of particular biblical writers or traditions.

For example, the Old Testament theologian may be interested in the covenant theology of the Yahwist (probably the
oldest of the several historical sources of the Old Testament).
He may compare or contrast this with priestly theology as
reflected in Leviticus, and with the theology of the prophets,
or of a particular prophet, say, Deutero-Isaiah or Amos. If
he is a New Testament theologian, he may be interested in
the theology of the synoptic gospels or of the general epistles.
He may compare the theology of the Fourth Gospel, John,
with that of the Apostle Paul. If the New Testament theologian has a historical inclination, he will probably seek to
show how the church's faith developed with the growth of
the early church. He may study, for example, the development
of Christology in the New Testament or the eschatology
of the church from the Book of Acts to the Apocalypse
(Revelation). In all of these studies the biblical theologian
will strive to combine scholarly integrity, a real "feeling" for
biblical faith, and a personal commitment.

Systematic Theology

When the average church member thinks of theology, he
probably has systematic theology in mind. Most studies of
doctrine in Protestant churches are in fact simplified courses
in systematic theology, and most Christian catechisms are
brief, systematic expressions of the church's theology. Indeed, catechisms themselves are usually elaborations of creeds,
which are more or less systematic and highly concentrated
expressions of the church's essential doctrines. Systematic

theology seeks to examine the expressions of faith with an eye toward completeness, so that no significant question concerning that faith is overlooked, and to do so in such a way as to make clear how the various doctrines of the faith relate to one another. While such a theology is greatly interested in men and movements in Christian thought, its organization is usually topical. It will examine the issues and allow specific theological men and movements to illustrate. If one were to look at the table of contents of any good book of systematic theology he would recognize there most of the subjects which have traditionally been the concern of Christian faith and preaching. Such an examination might give him a new appreciation for the scope and breadth of Christian faith in its theological expression. A typical systematic theology might have an outline something like the following.

 I. Theological knowledge and revelation (including the doctrine of Scripture)
 II. The doctrine of man
   A. Original righteousness (man's essential nature)
   B. The fall and the doctrine of sin
III. The doctrine of God
   A. God as creator (God the Father)
     1. God's transcendence
     2. The living God
   B. God as redeemer (God the Son)
     1. The incarnation (God becomes flesh)
     2. The person of Christ (as servant, Word, and Son)
     3. The work of Christ
       a. Cross and resurrection
       b. The atonement
   C. God as living presence (God the Spirit)
     1. The doctrine of the church
     2. The Christian life
     3. Sanctification
   D. The Christian hope (eschatology)

1. God and history
2. The consummation and end of history
3. The life everlasting

It should be kept in mind that the particular order of the topics is not essential, but such an outline does indicate an attempt to see each major concern as part of the whole of Christian faith and as intelligibly related to each other aspect of that whole. Indeed, the primary virtue of the systematic approach is that it forces us to see more wholly, and breaks us out of the tendency to build our theology exclusively on *one* aspect or a *few* aspects of the Christian reality and to ignore others equally vital. Most Christian heresies have resulted from an exclusive emphasis on one insight of faith or the experience of one individual or group to the exclusion of the rest. Such narrowness almost always results in distortion. Being systematic in our theology helps us to avoid narrowness and to see wholly.

Of course, the systematic theologian does not concern himself only with building great systems which include all heaven and earth. He often occupies himself with humbler projects, but when he works on a smaller scale the topical nature of his work is still evident. For example, a more modest work in this field might be the systematic exploration of the theology of a man or movement. He might also explore systematically the various aspects of a certain doctrine, as for example, Christology or the atonement.

It should perhaps be added that although in past centuries systematic theology has been the queen of the theological sciences, this is no longer so clearly the case. While its importance remains, it is probably not so popular a discipline as in the past. This is partly because of the historical orientation which has come to characterize almost all the liberal arts, but it is also partly because the task of "seeing wholly" has become such an awesome one today. The sheer mass of knowledge which has buried the modern world has made many

despair of getting the perspective necessary to tie it all together. As a result, many feel "banished from the land of
unity" which is the final aim of systematic theology. Few
systematic theologies are being written today and many seem
willing to express themselves in "theological fragments."
While such an attitude reflects a wholesome humility, it is
doubtful whether faith can finally escape the task of unifi-
cation. Indeed, the very profuseness of knowledge today makes
the effort to recover the unity of human existence before God
the more critical. And in fact the effort to unite all things
under God is not finally the goal of just systematic theology,
but of all theology and of faith itself.

Historical Theology

Historical theology is that approach which seeks to understand Christian thought in terms of its development. It is
genetic; that is, it is concerned with how Christian doctrine
came to be, its historical expressions and forms, especially as
they have been shaped by the cultural forces they experienced.
It differs from church history or history of Christianity in
that its concern is not so much with the events, institutions
and political involvements of the church as with the church's
changing thought about itself.

Historical theology is a relatively new approach to Christian
thought, at least as a formally recognized area of theological
method. Through most of Christian history the widespread
conviction that theology is unchanging ruled out a history of
doctrine. There might conceivably be a history of *heresy*,
but not of doctrine. This conviction that the beliefs were incapable of change was not peculiarly the outlook of faith regarding its truth. In fact, almost all sciences and areas of
knowledge presupposed the fixity of knowledge until fairly recent times. It is not surprising then that the church was at first
disturbed by the suggestion that theology, like everything else,
changes and develops through history. It was only in the late

eighteenth and early nineteenth century that man became really historical in the modern sense; that is, he became keenly aware of the reality of change, of the fact that we are immersed in a universe in process, and that we really understand nothing except in terms of time.

Today we study everything in terms of the processes which give it birth. Since 1900 all major areas of knowledge have become *genetic*, that is, have learned to refer all knowledge to its origins and to seek explanations of organisms, institutions, and men in terms of how they got that way. Astronomy became potentially genetic with Copernicus and actually so with Kant and the nebular hypothesis. Geology became genetic with Hutton and Lyle (who explained mountains, valleys, and ocean beds in terms of age-long natural processes), and biology became genetic with Darwin. In addition, a whole series of new sciences emerged which were genetic at heart, for instance sociology, archeology, and psychology. Each of these seeks to understand human culture, collective and individual, at least in part by examining the processes which made that culture the way it is.

Once Christians began to recognize the living variety of their faith and took seriously its human element, they were quick to see the value of a genetic or historical approach to theology. Therefore since the work of Friedrich Schleiermacher at the beginning of the nineteenth century, Christian theology had become increasingly historical in its orientation. It is probably safe to say today that most theological education both in Europe and America is basically historical. It is probably also safe to say that the most fruitful way for most lay people to begin to feel the heartbeat of Christian theology and to become personally involved in the theological life of the church is through a deepened awareness of the growth of that faith through the centuries.

Historical theology has its own special values to contribute to the development of a personal theology. It can make the

Christian aware of the rich variety and color of the theological traditions which have preceded him, and thus enrich his own faith and confession. Also, despite the variety of expression and the frequent hostility between theological perspectives within Christendom, it can make him aware of the deep unity of purpose and the broad elements of faith common to virtually all Christian fellowships. Furthermore, it can help him to overcome the "historical arrogance" of modernity and come to recognize the creativity, truth and contemporary value of that which has come to us from the past. Nothing is so revealing or so humbling as the discovery that the insights which we thought were exclusively the property of our generation were understood and given ever so vivid expression by the Luthers, the Thomases, or the Augustines of our past.

Christian Ethics

In contemporary theological education Christian ethics is usually considered a division of theology. It has, of course, an obvious practical extension in that it concerns the actual conduct and attitude of the Christian in the world. While as a theologian I would insist that the other theological disciplines are not without their practical expression, ethics is more explicitly directed toward application than, let us say, historical theology. For this reason it has often been considered a part of the practical field of religious study. Ethics as a theological discipline, however, is concerned with the *understanding* of Christian life which can be the basis for consistent conduct. It asks the questions concerning God, man, and the meaning of human history which must be answered before we can know how we should act in the world. Understood in this way, it clearly belongs to "Christian thought."

Ethics has an immediacy of appeal which the other disciplines probably lack, since we live every moment in the face of decisions. The question "What ought I to think?" is not quite so urgent as the demand, "What, in this crisis, am I to do?" Yet a sound Christian ethic always leads a person ultimately back to the prior questions which are theological.

These four areas, or approaches to theology, are not independent of each other. They necessarily interpenetrate; or to use another metaphor, they cross-fertilize one another, each making the other more fruitful. In the final analysis, they are different responses, which the believer—and the church—make to the reality of God in the living dialogue of faith. The lay theologian will not likely become an expert in any of them, nor will he even be able to read more than superficially in them, but he should be aware of the richness and flexibility open to him in his response to his faith.

A SURVEY OF THE HISTORY
OF CHRISTIAN DOCTRINE

In order for our discussion in subsequent chapters to be as useful as possible, it would be worthwhile to survey very briefly the history of the church's attempt to give expression to its faith. Nothing of comprehensive or detailed character is possible in the brief compass available to us. Again, our chief aim will be to catch a sense of the way in which Christian faith has emerged from a living conversation within the church and between the church and the world. Therefore we will try to characterize briefly the different periods of theological history and to indicate the primary concerns of the church as they gave rise to its doctrine.

The New Testament Period (Apostolic
Period, about A.D. 50 to 100)

Where does Christian theology begin? The answer is literally "at the beginning." This may be a truism, but it is also true. And it is hard for us today to grasp this fact, especially those of us who have grown up in the tradition of biblical literalism. We tend to make theological experts out of the disciples in the upper room waiting for Pentecost. Such was hardly the case. As Langdon Gilkey has reminded us, "These guys were pioneers." They look like old-timers to us. They wear beards and they speak Greek and Aramaic, and so they fool us. We are in reality the "old-timers," so incrusted by the barnacles of tradition that we can scarcely move. Any direction we go today someone is likely to pull out a tradition, wave it ominously in our faces, and warn us of heresy. These fellows were real beginners. There was no set theology. There had been no time for answers to the questions implied by faith. There had not even been time for the questions, for the most part, to be asked. Thus the theological situation at the beginning of the New Testament period was very fluid. Many possible directions lay open to the church in its attempt to understand and express its faith. Some directions would prove more adequate than others, but for the moment there was hardly any way to know what was heresy and what was not except by trial and error.

So, at the beginning practically no theology!—except for late Jewish theology, which, while useful in thinking through their Christian faith, was inadequate in many respects. Although most of the apostles were not trained theologians they seemed to understand instinctively that the old wineskins of Judaism were not capable of containing the new wine of Christ. What was there, then, for them to go on? What was there to become the core of a new theology? There was a tremendous and shattering event, an event which had shaken their world and transformed their sense of life. Through all of the church's early, often halting attempts to give expression to its faith shines the fact of its encounter with the man Jesus in his incredible life, death and resurrection. At first there was no theology, but only event.

Now this event had certain inherent implications which pointed toward theology, but there was no definite framework. This remained to be hammered out, and the process of hammering out an understanding of Christ and redemption was encouraged by the swiftness with which the church began to move out into an ever larger and more complex situation. Exposure of the church and its faith to the Palestinian-Judaic culture in which it was born and then within a short time to the rich extra-Palestinian Hellenism of the Mediterranean basin stimulated the development of its thought. As the church was confronted with the challenge of this stimulating and often hostile world, and as it felt the missionary responsibility of clarifying and communicating the meaning of the "Christ-event," the earliest "experiments" in Christian doctrine appeared. As differences of opinion began to arise the church found it necessary from time to time to eliminate some opinions as not doing full justice to the gospel, and so the ground began to narrow and a specifically Christian theology began to emerge. Often as one question was answered, it gave rise to new questions which the church then sought to answer in turn. Thus the history of doctrine sometimes takes on the appearance of a kind of systematic theology strung out through time. Each successful formulation raised new questions and led to the next formulation.

When the church began to "do theology" where did they get their content and the language and concepts for expressing that content? They derived the primary content of their theology from their experience of grace and from the common worship life of the church. In giving expression to it they used the language and concepts they found about them in their culture. This was both unavoidable and on the whole desirable. It was unavoidable because there was no other language available. It was on the whole desirable because the church must always address men in their own vocabulary and in terms of their own world view.

It is important for the reader to realize that all theology uses the language and thought forms of its culture, because as he becomes familiar with early Christian thought he will discover that the church borrowed ideas not only from Jewish theology but also from Greek philosophical thought and even from pagan sources. Such borrowing often comes as a shock to the believer, for it seems to deny the originality of the gospel and seems to reduce Christianity to the level of its sources. It is not necessary, however, to conclude that the gospel was compromised by the use of "cultural" language and ideas. Indeed, the fact that some categories of Greek thought were so useful in communicating the gospel seems providential. Paul himself on Mars' Hill quoted from Stoic sources, and other portions of the New Testament reflect Stoic, Gnostic and cultic influences. The critical question is how they used this cultural inheritance. In every case of conscious inheritance the church sought to transform these borrowed elements so that, purified of their foreign elements, they became adequate expressions for the gospel. In other words, the church sought to "baptize" cultural elements and make them Christian, just as every generation of theologians must do with its *own* cultural inheritance. Thus the Jewish Messiah became the suffering servant and the Stoic "logos" or world spirit became the personal "word" of God, Jesus Christ.

Of course, the process of transformation was not always complete. Sometimes part of the pagan meaning clung to an idea and crept unsuspected into the church. Sometimes a pagan or Greek idea could not be completely baptized and so persisted as a foreign body in the gospel, as in the case of Gnostic elements of world denial that Paul and John both struggled against. ("Touch not; taste not; handle not.") And so the church had to constantly be on its guard against heresy. Most of the early Christian heresies were untransformed cultural elements in the church, and a heretic was not one who imported ideas from surrounding culture into the church and its theology, but one who did so *without baptizing them.*

It is not difficult to see the parallel opportunity and danger which confronts the church today, and which particularly confronts the person who is seeking to develop his own theology. Our own culture is unequaled in richness and diversity, and offers many resources useful to faith. We are both tempted and compelled to employ these resources in shaping an adequate theology for our day. The resources of the business and advertising world, of modern physics and chemistry, of depth psychology, of existentialism and linguistics, of literature and the arts—these and many more offer themselves, *provided we can make them meaningfully Christian.* This is our continuing problem. How much of the culture of our day, and of its thought patterns and expression, is baptizable, and how much of it is inherently hostile to Christian faith?

Even in the New Testament we can see the process of exploration, expansion, borrowing and assimilation at work, and while there is much theological variety and difference of perspective among the various writers and different strata of its growing tradition, the impressive thing is how quickly a governing consensus—a common core of faith—began to emerge. Of special importance in this early faith was the message and proclamation of Jesus himself. Primary elements of his proclamation, as understood by the church, were (1) a fundamental belief in God as providential creator, righteous judge and loving father, (2) a stress on the Kingdom of God as the promised fulfillment of God's redemptive activity, and (3) the announcement of a citizenship and participation in that kingdom based on forgiveness and love. To the message of Jesus the church added elements which were not contained, except implicitly, in Jesus' proclamation. They were, in other words, able to say things about Jesus and about their faith which they could not have said until the cross, the resurrection and Pentecost were accomplished facts. For example, they sensed the profound (but little understood) significance of his death, and they understood that the last supper must be somehow central in expressing that significance. They also saw the resurrection as the confirmation of his mission, and as the decisive promise of victory over sin and death, so that it became the heart of the apostolic kerygma, or proclamation. In the light of Pentecost they came to see the church as the center of God's redeeming activity and the creation of a new kind of community on earth. Finally, they came to view the event of Christ as the assurance and promise of the fulfillment of human history in the *eschaton*, the "final appearance of Christ."

This much, at least, represents a common core of New Testament theology, and it is not an insignificant achievement given the brevity of the apostolic period and the constant expansion of the missionary situation. Much, however, was left undone. Many questions were inadequately answered or not answered at all, and these provided the content of theological controversy and development for subsequent centuries. Some of the central ones were as follows:

1. *The question of the Lord's return.* How was the *parousia* or the "promise of Christ's return" to be understood? Apparently most of the early Christians expected an almost immediate return of Christ, and were rather uninterested in the practical problems of living in the world. If he was due to return at once, there was little incentive for social ethics, for theology, or even for gainful employment. But as the century passed and Christ did not return, the question of the delay became inescapable. If Christ is not to return imminently, who was he, and what has he done, and how do we live in the world? As Paul seems to argue in 2 Thessalonians, ascension robes are not appropriate in the absence of an immediate parousia.

2. *The relation of Jesus to God.* The church had understood Christ to be the decisive and final revelation of God. "If you want to know what God is *really* like," they all agreed, "look at Jesus!" But who exactly was Jesus and what is the nature of his authority? Was he merely a man, a *prophet* perhaps, who spoke for God? Why then was he *final* and why did the church call him God's son? Was he more

than a man? If so, what? An angel? A second God? But Christians were monotheists! How could there be a second God without relapsing to polytheism? Out of this critical question came the trinitarian controversy, the first step in the formation of the Christian understanding of God.

3. *The relation of the divine and the human in Christ.* Once it was decided that Christ was truly God, the next question was obvious. "Why then call him man?" Was his humanity real or only a *theophany*, an "appearance" of being man? And if he is this, what does the *incarnation* mean, with its assurance that God really took on flesh for our sake and our salvation? The classic answer to these questions emerged from the smoke of theological controversy only after four hundred years of Christian history.

4. *The meaning of Christ's death.* It was understood generally that Christ's death was redemptive but not clearly how. This is the doctrinal question of the atonement. What is the death of Christ to God? Did God cause it? Did he *suffer* it? Is Christ's death alone atoning or is it only part of a redemptive life? What is its relation to man's sin? Is it a propitiation or satisfaction offered to God? A ransom paid to Satan? These and other questions remained to be explored.

5. *The problem of evil.* If God is good and sovereign, how did sin and evil arise? What is man's problem and how did he get that way? (These are the problems of creation and of anthropology.)

6. *The place of law in the Christian life.* Judaism had struggled long over the question of what place the law had in the covenant faith. Does a man achieve his place in the covenant by obedience to the law or does that place come as a gracious gift? The tension between law and grace which is reflected at times in the New Testament (for example, in Galatians) becomes a major issue in the post-Apostolic church. What is the place of law in the Christian life and

how does it relate to the reality of grace as the basis of our sonship?

7. *The problem of redemption, justification and sanctification.* It also remained for the church to explore the meaning and consequences of the redemption it had found in Christ. What is the result of redemption in the believer? The New Testament had made many fruitful suggestions and introduced rich analogies and figures to suggest the new life in Christ, but again it had provided no well-integrated understanding. What does it mean to be justified (Paul) and how does it relate to the life of regeneration (John)? How is a man changed by conversion? Does sin remain, or does the believer rise above sin in the new birth?

8. *The problem of sin in the life of the church.* In the first two centuries of the life of the church there was a strong tendency toward perfectionism. The church was generally held to be a holy community. This sense of sinlessness was encouraged by their awareness of contrast with the pagan world. Also, as long as they lived in momentary expectation of Christ's return, they were able to keep a modified but real sense of separation from the world. But with the nonappearance of the Lord and the necessity of rejoining the world— at least for gainful employment and for buying and selling —it became increasingly evident that they were still men. The grosser sins which they thought had been banished from the "holy community" now began to reappear. How was this fact to be understood? If believers sinned did they destroy the church as the holy community? And if they had been forgiven, could they sin and be forgiven again? Was forgiveness a once-for-all transaction or was the Christian life one of continuing forgiveness? Was the church a holy community or a community of sinners based on continuing mutual forgiveness and on the forgiveness of God?

Implied in this question was a question which was to be a significant one for the whole classical period of Christianity:

that of the relation of the church as the holy people to the sinful society about it. Should the church withdraw from society in order to remain unspotted from the world, or is its role one of involvement in order that it may sanctify, bless and redeem that society?

9. *The question of the relation of the church to the Kingdom of God and the end of time.* Apparently many in the New Testament period looked upon the time of the church as a brief interim period before the immediate consummation of history. Indeed, many assumed that death for Christians had already been swallowed up and ceased to be a threat. The problem they faced when believers began to die is reflected in 1 and 2 Thessalonians. When the last of the apostles died it became evident that the church was here to stay, and that the meaning of the present age, of death, and its relation to the eternal hope had to be rethought. Is the Kingdom, they asked, a present reality or do we look for it in the future? Is the church the foreshadowing of the Kingdom? Does the Kingdom come by preaching or by the radical breaking in of the end of time by the power of God? Does one go to be with God at death, or must he await a final resurrection at the end of time?

Now these questions and many more remained to be dealt with when the final writings of the New Testament came into existence. The New Testament often suggested directions for further thought but it remained for the church to seek fruitful and adequate formulations, and with the pursuit of such the history of Christian theology began. We can now survey the succeeding periods of Christian thought much more briefly.

The Classical Period (A.D. 100–500)

The church moves out into the world! The theological interests and achievements of this great formative period (also called the Patristic Period or the Period of the Fathers)

are significantly shaped by the church's moving out of the
ghetto of its Jewish origins into the mainstream of classical
life. At the beginning of the period it was a small, persecuted
band whose very survival seemed in doubt. Gradually, however, its missionary zeal and its toughness of character began
to make inroads into the classical culture, and by the end of
the period it had established itself as the religion of the empire. As the church began to win its way into Greek and
Roman society it was confronted by at least three practical
problems which helped to stimulate theological discussion,
and most of the theological controversy of this period reflects
these three problems.

There was, first of all, a crisis of authority. Although the
Apostolic church was by no means always *one* (as witness
the Judaizing and Gnostic sects with which Paul contended),
there was a basic unity of opinion and a common acceptance
of the theological and ecclesiastical authority of the apostolic
group. With the passing of the apostles, this consensus was
largely lost. Who *now* speaks for God, either on matters
theological or practical? It was commonly assumed that the
church must be one and if it lost its unity all else was lost.
Therefore the appearance of rival and heretical groups within
the church made urgent the development of a doctrine of
authority. The quick emergence of an authoritative canon of
Scripture, the development of creedal statements and the
emergence of a church structure (and an ecclesiology to justify
it) can be seen primarily as answers to the problem of disunity.

There was also an intellectual problem. The heart of the
gospel was the proclamation of God's activity in Jesus Christ.
As we have seen, such a proclamation carries with it difficult questions. So long as the church was mainly the church
of the lower classes, demands for intellectual consistency and
systematization were not great. But as the church began to
make converts in high places, it found itself challenged by
religious and philosophical views which were intellectually

far more sophisticated than Christianity. The church then found it necessary to begin to organize and clarify its message not only to answer the criticism of rivals, but to answer the questions raised by them in its own heart and to clarify for itself its proclamation. Most of the great theological controversies of the second through the fourth centuries reflect this struggle to understand clearly what they believed so passionately. It was during this period, therefore, that the great formulas emerged by which the church has through the centuries given expression to its unique insights into life, for example, its doctrine of God and its Christology.

Finally, the church faced a decision concerning its growing acceptance of and involvement with the world. Especially with the conversion of the Emperor Constantine in A.D. 325 and the establishment of Christianity as the religion of the empire, the Christians were forced to come to grips with the question of whether the holy church and the world are not inherently hostile to one another. There was reason to see the victory as the fruit of Christ's promises and as a rich opportunity to place the resources of empire behind the missionary enterprise. There was also reason to suspect that the world was by nature the enemy of God and that any alliance of church and empire, or any easy coexistence of the church and the imperial power was evidence that the church had sold its soul. The task of the church, said Tertullian, was to transform the world, not to sanctify it. Out of this controversy began to emerge differing theologies of the church. A consensus of sorts was reached in the fourth century, and given expression in Augustine's great theology of the church and the world entitled *The City of God*. It would hardly be an exaggeration to say that in Augustine, incomparably the greatest theologian of the Classical Period, and one of the few of the fathers equally claimed by Catholic and Protestant, the first period of doctrinal history was theologically summed up and concluded.

The Middle Ages (*about* A.D. *500 to about 1400*)

Faith seeks understanding! Augustine died with the Vandals at the gates of Hippo, thus symbolizing the death, at least in the West, of the Classical Era. But Augustine died with the faith that the "city of God," the church, was the only institution which had the power of survival in a dying order. He was right! And the vitality of the church in surviving the Fall of Rome and in eventually conquering and Christianizing the barbarian tribes which brought about that fall is the clue to its role in the medieval world. In medieval Europe all of life centered in the church. Not only religious truth, but virtually *every* value and vestige of the rich classical past came down to semibarbarian Europe through the church. There was no longer any serious question of alliance between empire and faith. Such alliance was a fact, and a *necessary* fact. Society rested on the basis of faith. The "city of the world" could not exist without the "city of God." There was, in the early Middle Ages at least, little real doubt that the vitality of society lay in the life-giving power of the church.

There was also little real theology, or at least little creative theology, for several centuries. This fact was mainly the result of the low level of understanding and of education resulting from the triumph of the relatively crude Teutons over the sophistication of Rome. So there was a marked drop in theological understanding from the sophistication of Augustine and Chalcedon, and it lasted almost five hundred years.

When a new and creative theology began to emerge, it still reflected this over-arching faith in the church. Theologians like Anselm of Canterbury and Bernard of Clairvaux never seriously questioned the reality of God and the truth of grace. It was in the very air they breathed. The life of the West was one culture lived under the sanctifying presence of God. This does not mean that there were no unanswered questions that called forth theology, but unlike the Classical

Period, they did not think of themselves as seeking to establish the faith against its rivals. There were no rivals. They
were seeking rather to make intelligible and understandable
what they already believed. Anselm took as his credo Augustine's formula that theology is "faith seeking understanding,"
and with such a stance scholasticism was born. Early scholasticism was far from stuffy and narrow; it was creative,
alive and fruitful. Most of the fundamental theology of the
Roman Catholic church took shape in this congenial atmosphere of faith in alliance with culture. Even when in the late
Middle Ages secularizing influences began to produce elements of thought and culture which seemed less tied to the
church, scholastic theology confidently set out to include
these also within the embrace of faith. Thus the Middle
Ages are summed up, both in tone and theology, in the great
system of Thomas Aquinas, which he appropriately called
the *Summa Theologica,* or "theological summary" of all
knowledge. Aquinas is still today the official theologian of the
Roman church.

The Breakup of Medieval Unity (1400–1600)

The great unity of faith and culture which was the Middle
Ages began to break up shortly after the medieval synthesis of
Aquinas was complete. The causes were many. Commerce
and industrial expansion produced a new middle class whose
independence unsettled the delicate feudal balance of noble
and peasant. World exploration and trade made European
culture aware of an outside world it had hardly known ex-
isted. Europe was breaking out of the ghetto. The rediscovery
of Greek classical culture, with its non-Christian and often
humanistic orientation, encouraged the growth of secular
culture within Christian Europe. The rise of the modern
national states gave a new focus for the loyalties and emotions
which had previously centered in the church. The overall result was the weakening of the place of the church and of

faith as a new, self-confident secular culture began to emerge.

The crisis for faith was very real. For the first time in a thousand years the church was faced by a rival world view and one which seemed to resist an easy baptism. How was it to respond? One response was to accept the outlook of the new humanism and to cut theology to its pattern. As a result, Catholic theology became in many areas moralistic, humanistic and rationalistic. Those who saw this as a surrender to a self-sufficient and shallow secularism sought a return to pre-scholastic theology. The Reformation was in large measure a repudiation of the modernism of the Renaissance and an attempt to reassert biblical and especially Pauline theology in relatively unmodified form. Out of the theological and social hostilities of the sixteenth century was born, for good or ill, not only modern Europe, but modern, denominational Christendom.

The Emergence of the Modern World
(1600 to the Present)

The breakup of medieval unity foreshadowed a change in culture and in man's understanding of his life unprecedented in human history. Its roots lie deep in the past, but it began to become clearly evident about the beginning of the eighteenth century and has continued to become ever more dominant in the past three centuries. It amounted to nothing less than a new world. The attitudes and outlooks of this new world were evident in the intellectuals of the eighteenth century, had spread to the educated middle class by the middle of the nineteenth century, and are the common property of all men in the West today. Therefore the "modern world view" is not really optional for us today; it is a "given." As the atmosphere of faith was to the Middle Ages, it is literally the "air we breathe." And since the biblical faith was created in a world view radically different from the scientific-humanistic one which began to emerge about 1700, Christian thought and life were confronted with tremendous problems. How was faith to be defended in an atmosphere increasingly indifferent or hostile? How was it to express itself in the face of a science so often at odds with traditional views of man, his universe and God? To a very large extent theology in the past three centuries has been done in response to the stimulating and often frightening challenge of this "big new world."

What are the dominant characteristics of the modern world view within which faith must make its way today? (1) It is first of all *rationalistic*. That is, it is committed to the fact that all reality must be in some sense understandable by man's rational powers. What is not rational in the broadest sense is not true. (2) It is also *empirical*. This means that for modern man reality is basically that which can be *experienced*, by the five senses or some extension of them. Now it is true that the rationalism and empiricism of the past three centuries have often been narrow and uncritical of their own limitations, but they have proved to be staggeringly successful in changing and shaping the world, as well as life in it. Empiricism is the method of science, and the incredible success of science in extending man's understanding and control of his world has put it largely beyond criticism. Most modern people accept without serious question the validity of the empirical principle. But if truth is empirical truth, how do you defend the reality of nontangible entities like God? (3) It is also scientific in its specific view of nature. The biblical faith was shaped in an ancient cosmology, in which man was the center of a finite universe of limited dimensions, both in space and time. The Bible reflects such an ancient geology and astronomy, and in medieval Christendom such a view was reinforced by Aristotle's philosophy. But increasingly science has created a new understanding of the world which seemed to conflict with this presumably biblical cosmology, casting doubt on the reliability of Scripture. (4) It is humanistic, optimistic and secular. The focus of values in the modern world has come increasingly to be human life as it is lived in this world. The otherworldliness of classical medieval times, undergirded by the brevity and poverty of life, has increasingly disappeared in the modern world. Life, lengthened by medical progress and enriched by modern culture, has become a value in itself and for many a completely adequate goal for living. Man today not only finds it difficult to believe in God, he often feels no special need for him as an answer to the problems of living.

It is against the backdrop of this rational, empirical, scientific and secular society that Christian faith and doctrine have sought to make their way. How are the Christian and the church to meet such a challenge? There are two basic responses always available. We can adapt our faith to the changing situation and seek to reinterpret the Christian confession in terms which modern men can understand, but always at the risk of losing vital elements of the gospel in the process, and of cutting the gospel down to terms acceptable to sinful men. Or we can oppose the cultural developments, refusing to alter our theology and our witness, relying on God to make it meaningful despite the differences of the biblical and modern outlook. But this alternative always carries with it the risk of becoming irrelevant and isolated from the real process of living. The church has tried both the "join-em" and the "lick-em" approach. Most nineteenth century theology represented an attempt to create a theology on the world's terms, to find empirical foundations for faith and to accept many elements of the modern world as good and worthy of approval. This movement, often called theological liberalism, was very creative, and has deeply influenced almost all theology of the twentieth century. However, it sometimes proved to be too naïvely humanistic and optimistic and therefore open to disillusionment and abuse. Thus beginning about 1914 a reaction against liberalism appeared under the leadership of Karl Barth in Germany. It attacked man's optimistic and self-centered adequacy and sought to recover the biblical proclamation in its primitive terms. It rejected the role of reconciling faith with culture. The task of the church, it asserted, is not to argue but to proclaim. This movement, often called neoorthodoxy, proved to be a powerful regenerative force in theology up to about 1950, but it now seems to have lost much of its force because of its essentially negative attitude toward the world.

In a very real sense this is where the church and the believer stand today: in the world, of the world, seeking to make their faith intelligible and urgent to that world (and to themselves as a part of it), seeking to make it also true to the Christian confession which has been born in past ages and in their own soul by the living power of God.

SUGGESTIONS FOR THOUGHT
AND DISCUSSION

1. Does the suggestion (pp. 118–19) that the apostolic group at first had little theology bother you? Why? What does this say about your understanding of theology?

2. It is suggested above that new experiences forced the church to recast its theology. Have you had an experience which forced you to reevaluate some element of your theology? Discuss it with your group.

3. On pp. 123–26 are important theological questions which confronted the early church. Which of these are still significant for you and your fellowship? Are some relatively meaningless or uninteresting? Why do you think this is so?

4. How do you react to the suggestion that the church borrows language and ideas from the world? Why?

5. Are there areas of modern life and thought which you feel could contribute to faith? In what ways? Would their contribution need to be modified or "baptized"?

CHAPTER EIGHT

Understanding Yourself
(Theological Anthropology)

WHERE DO WE START in filling in the content of a personal theology? In principle there is no right starting place, since every area of our experience is a part of a whole life lived in the world before God. And as we have seen, if our theology is fruitful, wherever we start we will find ourselves led immediately to ask about the other concerns of life and faith. It is logical to begin theology by talking of God, and theology has traditionally begun with the doctrine of God; but to ask about God is to immediately wonder about man. The psalmist reflects the inseparable character of these two concerns when he declares "O Lord our Lord, how excellent is thy name. . . . When I consider . . . the work of thy fingers . . . what is man, that thou art mindful of him?" If we begin with God, as Christians we soon find ourselves inquiring about Christ as God's self-manifestation. If, on the other hand, we begin with Christ, as in a sense every Christian theology must, we are moved to ask at once, "What manner of man is this, that even the winds and the sea obey him," and thus are driven back to the questions of man and God. If we start with the church as that reality in which our Christian life begins and our faith flourishes, then all the implied questions about God and Christ are not long in arising. And Paul Tillich has told us, ironically but accurately, that we could even begin theology with eschatology (the doctrine of "last things") since at its heart is a concern for the final meaning of human history under God. Therefore our choice of a starting point is to some extent a matter of convenience or practical organization.

THE IMPORTANCE OF YOUR
DOCTRINE OF MAN

Our survey of the major areas of Christian theology begins with an examination of the doctrine of man. The theologian speaks of this area of his concern as theological anthropology, from the Greek *anthropos,* or "man." There are two rather practical reasons why we choose this point of departure. First, we all really start here. This is descriptive of the actual process by which a person comes to the life of faith and to the task of theology. Wherever else we go, or wherever we start in writing down our theology, we actually begin *as men,* aware of ourselves, our relations, our problems, our fears and our hopes—and this is the stuff of anthropology. Theology is the answer which faith gives to the deep and perplexing questions of our existence. In other words, theology arises out of the existential situation of life. At the root of every theological expression is an unspoken question about what it means to be a man.

This fact is reflected in the history of Christian thought. Every important step forward theologically was born out of the agony of human need and the attempt to understand life in the light of that need. Paul Tillich has reflected this "life-centered" character of theology in his own description of theological method, which he calls the "method of correlation." He points out that, properly speaking, every doctrinal statement has two elements, a question which arises out of the human situation and an answer which is spoken by faith through revelation. This is reflected in the five-part structure of his own theology, namely (1) Reason and Revelation, (2) Being and God, (3) Existence and the Christ, (4) Life and the Spirit, and (5) History and the Kingdom of God.

In each case, the first term of the pair expresses the problem which confronts man in his existence and the second is the word of faith to it. For instance, to be a man is to be a rational creature, to strive for knowledge or understanding and to long to know the truth. Yet it is also to know that reason always breaks up into frustration and irrationality and final truth always slips through our fingers. Faith's answer to the question, "Why is it so?" is that somehow the broken-ness of reason and the elusiveness of truth can only be healed by a word of grace spoken to us by God—in other words, by revelation. The answer to the frustrating insecurity of being, with its constant threat of nonbeing, of disintegration and death, is *God*, who is the ground of being, the one who is not threatened by death and in whom we also are freed from its terrors. The answer to the brokenness of my existence is the one who brings healing and reconciliation, namely Christ. The answer to the question of the plurality of life, its con-fusing multiplicity and conflict is the one who brings unity out of chaos and makes life a whole, namely the Spirit. Finally the answer to the longing of the human heart for a fulfillment which ever eludes us here is the promise of the Kingdom of God. Thus in every case the central confessions of the Chris-tian faith ("I believe in God the father . . . and in Jesus Christ his son . . . and in the Holy Spirit") are spoken to the felt needs of human existence.

It should be pointed out that I am not arguing for Tillich's particular theological structure, or even for his method as such. But it seems clear that he is expressing a fundamental fact of great importance for the lay theologian, namely, that all theology is "answering theology," and that behind every confession is a question about what it means to be a man. "I waited for the Lord; he inclined unto me." If my theology is to be meaningful to me as a Christian, it must speak to the man that I am and answer the questions I am asking myself. If it is to be meaningful to other men, it must likewise speak to them in their situation and to the felt needs that for them define what it is to be men. Nothing is more irrelevant than a theology which goes about answering questions that nobody is asking. Therefore the task of Christian anthropology is to discover the real questions at the heart of our situation and to express them in such a way as to elicit response and recognition.

If all theology is answering theology then we have a second reason for beginning with man, namely, that a person's understanding of man will determine everything else in his theology. The way in which you understand the problems and distortions of the human situation will determine your diagnosis and your recommendations for treatment. The attempt to analyze the problem of the human situation constitutes what we might call the negative side of anthropology. And since diagnosis influences treatment, your doctrine of man sets limits for the more positive work of theology. If the trouble with man lies in his environment, then "salvation" may consist of a new social order (as in communism). If the trouble is biological then a new serum or biological engineering may be the answer. If his trouble is rebellion against God and alienation from others and from himself, then the answer may be in terms of reconciliation. Your understanding of man will also influence your hopes and expectations. This is the positive side of anthropology. If man is no more than a naked ape, then his potential for overcoming animal hostilities and achieving fulfillment and blessedness will be limited to the possibilities inherent in "animalhood." If in significant respects he is unique among the creatures of the cosmos, then speculation about his future potential may be of an entirely different sort. Whatever *answer* a person is able to hear with seriousness, and what he dismisses as absurd, is likely to be determined by his understanding of what it is to be man, whether that understanding is uttered or unexpressed.

The fact that men hear the gospel in the light of their own anthropology may help to explain why a type of theology or a manner of preaching which is effective in one time or with one group may not be effective under different circumstances. A subtle change in the view of man commonly held may make the particular language of our preaching seem to miss the point. For instance, most of the theology of the Reformation period is addressed to people who for one reason or another had a deep sense of sinfulness. The brokenness of human life was expressed in a feeling of alienation from God. Thus when Calvin spoke of each man's rebellion against the gracious love of God, men understood what he meant, whether they responded to his demands or not. The language of sin, judgment and forgiveness made ready sense. The men of Luther's day did not have to wrestle quite as we do with the idea of "total depravity." They understood instinctively what it meant. It has been argued, not without reason, that twentieth century man has a less intense sense of sin than sixteenth century man possessed, or at least that the word *sin* no longer expresses for him his sense of being a man. If this is the case it does not mean that the experience of sinfulness is no longer a part of life, but it does suggest that a new way of expressing the human situation may be called for and a new way of proclaiming the gospel as God's word of grace may be required. Perhaps in one situation the dominant motif is sin and salvation, in another brokenness and healing, or purposelessness and divinely revealed purpose. In any case, the understanding of man we hold shapes significantly our understanding of salvation.

I suspect that many of the practical difficulties confronting the church, especially in its struggle to make its message arresting and convincing, lie in its failure to sense subtle changes in man's understanding of himself and to adjust its proclamation accordingly. It is in this area that the lay theologian can be of unusual value to the church, since he lives in intimate contact with men. He is not insulated by the specialized nature of his work or by a ministerial status, and is in a position to correct the sometimes too theoretical anthropology of the academic theologian. Tillich himself was criticized for letting his theological prejudices shape the questions, so that his answers were sometimes more suited to the questions he would *prefer* that men ask than to the ones they were actually asking. If he is guilty, he is not alone in his guilt. My teacher Langdon Gilkey has told of the revealing remark of Dr. John Randall, the Cambridge pragmatist and historian of thought who served on Dr. Gilkey's doctoral committee. After sitting silently through Gilkey's final oral examination in which a number of theological issues were debated, Dr. Randall was asked to comment. "My only impression," he responded, "is that theologians are best equipped to answer the kinds of questions that theologians like to ask." This ironic criticism is not without point. What is the real "human situation" today? Part of the seeming irrelevance of much theology of the past may reflect the absence of the sensitive lay theologian, able to sense the real mood of man, able to detect the real questions and to call the professional theologian back to reality.

What we have been saying might seem to imply that we are to shape our theology to man's own requirements and that we are to say nothing at all that he is not prepared and willing to hear. If this were the case then there would be no gospel, no "good news" to be spoken to man and certainly no word of judgment. While our theology must speak to man *as he is,* it must speak as the word of judgment and also of promise. The questions may be asked by man in his situation, but the decisive answering of the questions must come from God. Thus the Christian again lives in tension between his "human-all-too-human" situation and the word of redemption through Christ. The Christian theologian lives with one foot in the circle of faith and one foot in the world. He seeks to be true to his experience as a man and to honestly hear what other men say about *their* manhood, and he also seeks to be true to the word of God *to* man. To ignore the former is to court irrelevancy. To neglect the latter is to cease to be Christian.

THE RAW MATERIAL FOR A DOCTRINE OF MAN

We have spoken above of the human situation or human experience as the source of man's self-understanding. Now, obviously the human situation is in some respect unique for every man. No two persons can share the same experience, and a good anthropology will stress this uniqueness. Nevertheless, a doctrine of man is an attempt to discover, understand and describe the qualities and dimensions common to all our particular experiences—that is, to discover what it is to be a man. In the past it was common to speak of human nature in describing this shared core of human experience. This term has recently fallen under suspicion, since it seems to suggest a permanence and unchangeability in man which is not too congenial with the best evidence today. Whatever man is, he is not frozen into rigidity by something abstract in him called his nature. He may have become what he is by growth and change and he may in the future become more—or less—than he is today. Nevertheless, *human* means something not necessarily exact but surely real, and we cannot help generalizing on what it is to be a man. The theologian knows that all men *have* an anthropology. He is concerned to present to man an understanding of himself which is both convincing and apt to open the way to a hearing of the gospel.

It is important to understand that the Christian's raw material for a doctrine of man is the same as that available to everyone else, whether he be a sociologist, a black militant, a Communist, a Freudian psychoanalyst, or a serene secularist. If the Christian's anthropology is to be persuasive it must make intelligent sense of the common experience of men. If the Christian's doctrine of man is different from other anthropologies, the difference does not lie in a different source, since the Christian shares the experience of being a man with others. The difference must lie instead in a superior clarity with which he sees the underlying issues, and in an honesty and inclusiveness growing out of his experience of grace.

What are some of the common elements of human experience with which we need to deal in a doctrine of man? What does it mean to be a man? Perhaps nothing is more characteristic of human experience than its *polarity*. By this expression is meant its tendency to be expressed in opposites, or its quality of being in tension between seeming contradictories. Almost everything that has been said about man in traditional thought has reflected this polar quality, and most of the characteristic problems in understanding man have arisen out of the fact that he can adequately describe his experience only by contrasts. Man is of nature, yet over and above nature; he is determined by his environment and history, yet free to determine it; he is good, yet evil; he is the union of love and hate, of creativity and destructiveness; he is the most fully mortal of creatures with a taste (and capacity?) for immortality. And any honest and adequate doctrine of man must do full justice to this polar character.

It is important to understand that polarity does not mean merely that man is partly one and partly the other. It affirms that experientially he is one person, yet in eternal tension between these two dimensions of his nature. Nor does it mean that he is the happy medium between the two and therefore partly free and partly determined, partly hatred and partly love, and so forth (like the proverbial man with his feet in ice and his head in an oven, being on the average comfortable). Such thinking leads usually to the division of man into two parts—body and soul—the former determined, the latter free, the former mortal, the latter immortal. Such a deceptively easy solution has no justification either in modern science or in Scripture. To be a man is to be *all these at the same time,* and in such a way that to affirm one is to be driven to affirm its opposite as well.

Since it is difficult for most men to live in tension between opposites, and since the laws of traditional logic have made little provision for the polarities of life, we often escaped the paradox by belittling or ignoring one or the other of the polarities. Anthropology has proven an easy victim to the error of reductionism. This results when one aspect of the polarity is affirmed and the other rejected as illusion because it cannot be made to rest comfortably with the first. For example, materialism affirms the natural origin of man and denies that he is in any decisive way above nature, while philosophical idealism and some Christian theology has discounted or denied that the physical in man is real or significant, identifying man with pure soul. While most Christians would feel more comfortable with the latter view, it must be emphasized that both are equally reductionistic and achieve their attractive simplicity only at the expense of truth.

The polar quality of which we have spoken runs through all the aspects of human experience and accounts for both the unique possibilities and the shattering frustrations of human life. Although the expressions mentioned above do not exhaust the polarities of life, they are perhaps the classic forms in which our polar nature confronts us, so a fuller comment is called for.

Of Nature and above Nature

Man is a creature who is rooted in the natural order. His chemical constitution is identical with that of other organisms and, with differences of proportion, the same as that of nature and of the earth which is his home. His kinship with nature and his dependence on the natural order for his survival is one of the most primitive awarenesses of men. And this awareness has been reinforced in a most impressive way in the past two hundred years by almost all the sciences. Biological developmentalism has reduced the gulf between man and the animals both genetically and qualitatively. Psychology and physiology have demonstrated the dependence of consciousness and personhood on the physical organism, pointing to the fact that chemical and physical alterations in the body can produce substantial alterations in personality. The whole of life is lived in an environment whose radical alteration would doom not only the individual but the race. Whereas only a few hundred years ago both the origin and destiny of men were understood to be extra-natural and his immersion in nature temporary and nonessential, today man's natural character is all too painfully apparent. Whatever else we are, we are dependent children of this natural order.

It is sometimes tempting and convenient to think of man as merely a higher anthropoid who by accident of environment or of evolution (for example, the social necessity of plains survival or the upright posture and opposable thumb) has succeeded, where the apes and the dolphin have failed; but such a position can scarcely be true to the facts. Man's *difference*, for all his similarity, is greater than all that. Quite apart from the question of its source, the raw fact of human experience is that while man is in and of nature he is in significant ways able to rise above his natural origin. It is scarcely important whether we describe the difference as one of degree or of kind. (A. N. Whitehead has said that a difference in degree, carried to a sufficient magnitude, becomes a difference in kind!)

Part of what it means to be a man is to be able to transcend the given order and create a new order. Man does this first of all in his capacity for thought. Although mental processes, sometimes of a high order, are certainly evident in the animal world, man only has been able through conceptual thought to escape the limitations of time and place which, so far as we can tell, largely limit the highest animals. Man is the animal who can contemplate past and future and bind them together by resolution. He is able in thought to escape spatial limitations and therefore contemplate places unseen and deeds undone. In acting he transcends his order by creating a new order. Only man has a history which he has grafted onto nature. This is perhaps his most visible difference from even the most intelligent animal forms. Dolphins, despite the complexity and sophistication of their brains, seem to have been capable only of those changes which evolution has worked in them. They owe their heated aquariums to the ingenuity of men. Man has been changed by nature, much like the dolphin, or the socially well-organized and highly intelligent forest gorilla, but he has also by deliberate and purposeful action changed nature. I write these words in a refreshed awareness of what it means to be a man and with a renewed sense of the difference between my own species and the other animals. The date is July 21, 1969. Less than twenty-four hours ago the first men in history broke through the limitations of nature and stood on the surface of the moon. Perhaps no single achievement in human history has made it so clear that man, for good or evil, is more than nature.

So it is man's destiny to be both of nature and over it, and any adequate doctrine of man will recognize this fact, and it will also acknowledge the complexity and ambiguity in man's existence which this polarity implies. Each time the materialist or the naturalist seeks to dismiss man as no more than nature, his unique role in and over nature must be reaffirmed. Each time the humanist is tempted to make man more than nature—indeed, more than God and the measure of all values and all things—he must be reminded that man is not God, but a part of the world.

Determined and Free

What has been said above implies a certain freedom of man in the world and with regard to the world. Indeed, almost every social definition of man will speak of his freedom. To deprive a man of his freedom is to deprive him of his manhood. Yet the problem of freedom is one of the knottiest problems with which men have wrestled in coming to understand themselves, for to be a man in the world is to know that one is shaped and conditioned by all the natural and social forces which he experiences. "I am a part of all that I have met," said Tennyson's Ulysses, and indeed the "I" which I am so concerned with preserving as free has no identity except in the relations which determine and shape me. "Who am I?" I am father, son, husband, teacher, friend, colleague; and all of these relations determine my being. Further, I am this body, these atoms, this hormone imbalance and that undigested frankfurter which denied me my freedom through a sleepless night. "A man is what he eats," said Feuerbach. We do not hesitate to admit that an animal is at the mercy of its environment—the weather, the food supply, the mating instinct. Is it not the same in the case of man? Can we not indeed give a kind of place to freedom even in a deterministic anthropology by defining it as that *feeling* of satisfaction when I am allowed to be *myself*, even though I am determined to be that self? Freedom would then not be freedom to create the new, to act contrary to my environs or to choose one option out of many, but merely freedom from external constraint.

Such an understanding of freedom would be compatible with a mechanical determinism and has been attractive not only to naturalists and materialists, but also to a great many Christian theologians. Yet it is extremely difficult to consistently reduce human freedom to these terms. It has a way of reasserting itself in the practical attitudes and ethical presuppositions of the most committed determinist. I have a friend who is a mechanistic materialist. He sometimes becomes very unhappy with me for my naïve persistence in speaking of freedom, yet on his own principle, as I point out to him, I must be determined in such a belief and in no way to blame for it. Nor is he happy with my teasing explanation that no doubt he is determined to be irritated with me and likewise not to blame. He is sure that his position—freely chosen—is right. The assumption of real freedom, as Kant pointed out, seems to be essential for every judgment of value and for every ethical or moral decision, and surely moral and ethical judgments are uniquely human. Indeed, the moral integrity of the determinist seems to be dependent on freedom.

It is a popular ploy of the theologian to attack the materialist at this point of practical inconsistency, and I am not attempting to deny the very real truth of determinism, but to make clear that it expresses only one pole of the human dilemma. To be a man is to be free *even though* determined and determined *even though* free. This is what it *means* to be a man. If a simple determinism is false to experience, so is a simple doctrine of absolute freedom. I am *not* free to be anything. My freedom is limited and *shaped creatively* by its limits. In fact, it is quite inconceivable to me what absolute freedom could be. It might in fact be hell. Therefore, any faithful and convincing doctrine of man must do justice to this polarity.

Good and Evil

The polarity of human existence is expressed most poignantly in the tension between good and evil. This tension is expressed not only in the ambiguity of individual existence but also in the agony of history. Whereas the animals are neither good nor evil, but simply what they are, man is the creature who is capable of the loftiest worth and the most complete perversion; and these two aspects of his existence, in true polar fashion, are inseparable. It is his capacity for goodness which sets him above the beasts, and also that which makes him capable of the most exquisite corruption. If he could not love—himself, others, and God—he could not hate. Creativity and destructiveness go so hand in hand that behind every new weapon of war lies the admirable imagination and creative skills of men of good will.

One's evaluation of man—whether, for example, the good is more basic or the evil—will largely determine his hopes for history and his attitude toward culture. The optimist affirms the good, the creative element, because he takes seriously man's capacity for altruism and for love, and sees the future in the light of men's affirmative possibilities. And in so doing he is in touch with truth. But a simple optimism obscures truth. It must close its eyes to evil, and therefore is open to the most devastating disillusionment. To a considerable extent this was the fate of early twentieth-century liberalism—both social and religious—which dismissed the evils of society as evolutionary and cultural hangovers to be soon outgrown. It was therefore unprepared for the incredible agony of two world wars and their aftermath. Liberalism has never quite shaken off the brute facts of Auschwitz and Hiroshima. It is the capacity of man to sour even his most worthy achievements which is the impulse to pessimism. A cynical view of man which makes his capacity for evil dominant is an understandable response to the tragedy of human existence. Yet it is also a naïve reductionism, for it ignores the altruism of which man is capable and cannot account for his unwillingness to affirm tragedy. The judgment we pass on the evil of our existence—and most especially on our own evil—is evidence that man is more than evil.

So once again, neither an optimism which obscures evil nor a pessimism which stifles and restricts love and creativity is adequate to man. He is too complex a being for optimism or pessimism. He is neither angel nor demon, but he is somehow both. He points the way to heaven and to hell. He is "polar" man.

Mortal with a Taste for Immortality

Perhaps the dilemma of man is expressed most vividly in his polar relation to the eternal. Man, like other creatures, combines being and nonbeing. He has existence, but his existence is tenuous and fragile. He can cease to be. But unlike other creatures, man is *aware* of his finitude. This awareness in a sense raises him above that finitude, for unlike the angels, he can contemplate both death and the conquest of death. Yet he cannot conquer death. In this condition he is both more lofty and more lowly than any other creature known to him. Because he is more than the animals he can dream of fulfillment and blessedness, peace and immortality, but because he can dream of these, he can also dream of death. He becomes the creature who lives each moment of his life in the fact of his mortality. He can know a blessedness and an agony unknown to beast or angel. It is reserved for man. He is polar man.

THE MEANING OF TRADITIONAL ANTHROPOLOGY

We have been describing man's situation without special reference to the traditional biblical and Christian understanding, although it has been in the back of our minds. This is true both because the writer is a theologian and can't cut himself off from his roots and because the biblical view of man has so deeply influenced our whole culture. We need now to see briefly how man has been represented in traditional Christian thought, in order that we may draw on these insights when they are useful and to possibly modify or change them when our own theological outlooks require it.

Biblical anthropology and the church's doctrine of man have been by no means monolithic. One can find a wide spectrum of opinions about man in the biblical material and also in the history of the church. Perhaps the most persistent quality throughout, however, has been a stubborn determination to preserve the polar quality of which we have spoken. This polarity is reflected vividly in the epic of creation in the first three chapters of Genesis. These chapters are in effect an essay on anthropology, since their center of concern throughout is man, his origin, his dilemma, and—at least in anticipation—his hopes. Chapters one and two describe the creation of man as a part of his world. Chapter three tells the story of the fall and thereby sets out the nature of man's problem. The church has usually followed this outline and divided its doctrine of man into two doctrines, creation and sin.

The Meaning of the Doctrine of Creation

The doctrine of creation is not primarily concerned with questions of cosmic origins but with questions of human meaning. It is a commentary on the purpose and goal of existence. The source of that meaning is God, and its focus is man. The doctrine of creation affirms that man is in some sense central to the meaning of existence. He is its climax and goal of creation (Genesis 1) or he is God's prime creation (Genesis 2). Both point to the centrality of man in creation and all Christian theology has affirmed, in various ways, this centrality.

Implied in the biblical doctrine of creation are certain basic affirmations:

1. *The value of man.* By his act of creation, by the special place accorded to man in it, and above all by his entering into fellowship and covenant with man, God has affirmed the essential worth of man. Therefore for the Christian, respect for selfhood has been rooted not in some idea of inherent human worth—he is like all else a part of nature—but in the expressed concern and love of God. This means that selfhood is to be respected as one respects and values God.

("Thou shalt love the Lord thy God . . . and thy neighbor as thyself.")

2. *The goodness of man.* Throughout the story of creation it is affirmed repeatedly that "God saw that it was good." No affirmation is more central than this to biblical faith. It sets Hebrew-Christian faith against those philosophies and cosmologies which hold that any aspect of reality is fundamentally evil or opposed to the fulfillment of God's purpose. There is nothing in creation which did not come from the hand of God and therefore nothing can finally resist or frustrate his purpose. Thus Christianity is basically world-affirming and opposed to every dualism. This is the case whether we are confronted with ancient Gnosticism and Manichaeism or their modern equivalents—for example, atheistic existentialism, which affirms the moral absurdity of the cosmos.

As the climax and goal of a good creation man is also good. This means that there is nothing inherently wrong with him. In this sense his evil is less ultimate than his good. And what this really means is that he is redeemable. It is an eschatological doctrine, like the entire doctrine of creation; it is not just an affirmation of how we began but also of what we can hopefully become. Since man is in his nature good, he is despite his sin worthy and capable of salvation and of fellowship with God. The doctrine of creation "looks not toward Eden but toward the Kingdom of God."

3. *The uniqueness of man.* According to Genesis man is in the *image of God.* Now the significance of this graphic phrase has been variously understood in theological history, but it seems clear that its biblical intent was to express man's difference from the animals and to set him off from the rest of creation. However rooted in nature, according to Genesis he has a unique place in nature. This idea is expressed by the concept of dominion. Man is to "get dominion" over the birds of the air and the beasts of the field. The consequence of his dominion is the creation of his own world and his own

history. Thus man is uniquely like God; he is both Lord of creation and a kind of creator in his own right. Only man, in his freedom, brings forth the new. He is, by virtue of the image of God in him, a co-creator with God.

4. *The dependence of man.* Being in the image of God affirms that man is a creator, but this creativity is good only as it is exercised under God. Man is the *image* of God, not God. Because of his free creativity and his lofty place in the universe, man is tempted to ignore this difference and to exercise his dominion on his own. If *like* God, why not *be* God! Indeed, the fall of man is precisely his desire to "become like God, knowing good and evil." So his unique status once again becomes both his possibility and his temptation. If he exercises dominion under God he contributes to the unity and wholeness of life. In fellowship with God everything in life is congenial (the garden). If he rejects this dependence he does not cease to have this free creativity but he brings forth evil.

It is sometimes suggested that the biblical doctrine of dominion is responsible for the corruption of nature and the spoiling of the human environment. It is certainly true that in the West nature has been viewed as not in itself sacred but available to man for his use and development. It is possible that modern technology could never have been achieved without such a view. On the other hand, the doctrine of the image of God not only offers man dominion but solemnly warns of its danger. It is a two-edged sword. And the kind of exploitation which threatens to render the earth a cosmic garbage heap and to pollute the environment beyond survival is not the *expression* of dominion but its corruption. It is a part of the doctrine of sin.

Thus the doctrine of creation has affirmed both the value of man (and the compatibility of that value with the nature of things in general), his uniqueness, his creativity and freedom, and finally, his redeemability. This is the fundamental truth about man.

The Meaning of the Doctrine of Sin

What has been said about man is true but it is not the whole truth. Man may be ideally good, free and creative but existentially he is also evil, enslaved and destructive. How did he get that way? The biblical answer is the fall and the theological answer is the doctrine of sin. Whether expressed in terms of the disobedience of our first parents or in language descriptive of universal experience, the aim of the doctrine of sin has been to account for the tragic dimension of human experience and to ask about its significance for man. Traditional doctrines of sin have varied widely in their form, but have usually agreed in affirming the reality and seriousness of sin, thus warning against a deceptive optimism. They have also agreed, however, that sin is not final or ultimate but exists to be overcome by the redemptive activity of God. Thus cosmic pessimism is ruled out for the believer.

The meaning of the Christian doctrine of sin could perhaps be summarized in two basic affirmations. First, it expresses our recognition of the human capacity for self-destruction and "other-destruction," which in some respect grows out of our freely chosen rejection of God. Second, it is a confession of the resulting incompleteness of life in separation from him. To be a sinner is to live in loneliness. It is to exist in separation from God, from others, even from ourselves. Therefore the doctrine of sin is the overture to the doctrine of redemption.

THE MODERN WORLD AND ITS IMPLICATIONS FOR A DOCTRINE OF MAN

We have said above that changes in man's understanding of himself can have deep impact on theology, since the word of redemption must be spoken to man as he is. Thus in a world changing as rapidly as our world has changed during the last two centuries, the intelligent Christian must seek to be sensitive to social and technological alterations which affect modern man's anthropology. It is probably true that man's self-image has undergone more and deeper modifications since 1900 than in the previous fifteen hundred years, and each of these changes will have its effect on the way in which we shape and express our theology. I can only mention a few of the major questions raised for a doctrine of man by this big new world.

The Problem of Human "Nature"

We have already commented on the questionable status of the concept of human nature. If in fact man's nature has developed by degrees from prior forms of life, as is suggested by biology today, then it becomes more difficult to distinguish human nature from the rest of nature. Furthermore, theology has usually assumed in the past that all men shared the same basic "man-ness," thus making the same gospel able to be spoken to all men, perhaps with the same tone and emphasis. What if this is not so? What if the essential qualities of selfhood differ from culture to culture and even from man to man? What bearing does this have on theology? Most significantly, perhaps man is still in the process of change, a process intensified by technological and medical progress. Today's talk of biological and genetic engineering holds forth the possibility of future generations significantly different in native abilities as well as in psychological make-up. What if a man could be bred who, tranquillized chemically, lives his life without the anxiety of death? How would the gospel speak to him?

The "Dethronement" of Man

As we have seen, biblical anthropology looked upon man as the center and goal of creation and redemption. The value in which personhood has been held in western culture has rested heavily upon this belief that man is, of all creation, the unique being in the image of God. And it was not difficult to accept the accuracy of this valuation as long as the old Ptolemaic cosmology still prevailed. Until the sixteenth century man was king upon the earth, and the earth stood at the very center of the universe, with sun, moon and the galaxies encircling it. Furthermore, in the premodern time scheme cosmic history was almost identical with human history. Creation and time itself came into being as a cradle for man. As one writer put it in awed respect, "Time is but five days older than we!"

But almost every major development in modern science has tended to push man increasingly from the center of things. From Copernicus' time our earth has shrunk to an inconceivably small and insignificant mote in the universe—lovely, blue and alone. The whole of human history is now seen as the last hesitant tick of an almost inconceivably vast cosmic time. Furthermore, whatever sense of centrality and uniqueness nineteenth century man had managed to cling to by virtue of the doctrine of special creation has now been challenged by evolutionary biology. The real shock of Darwin was not that he was the first step in challenging the scientific accuracy of the Bible; this challenge was at least as old as Copernicus. Darwin represented the last step in a new anthropology which demoted man to the level of the rest of nature.

In all, modern man is finding it difficult to believe that it is not arrogance to suggest that human purpose and human destiny are of real and final importance. If once man was too arrogant in his own self-esteem, he seems to be threatened today with a devastating inferiority complex. How can a Christian theology speak to man in this mood, or how can it make use of other developments—space achievement, perhaps —to help man recapture a sense of significance?

Problems Raised by Technology and Science

There are implications for anthropology in many aspects of the contemporary technological revolution. Cybernetics and computer technology promise the development of machines which in ever greater completeness reproduce the physical and mental activities of man. Not only are we faced with the very real possibility of "computer revolt" visualized in science fiction, but the development of automated and electronic creations able to simulate human processes so closely that no theoretical difference can be discovered. Do such machines thereby become persons? Or, perhaps more troubling for religious faith, does this suggest that man is no more than a highly complex bioelectronic machine?

Medical progress has also raised questions about man. The demonstration of the dependence of personality on bodily function not only raises questions of moral responsibility and sin, but also makes it difficult for many to take seriously the independence of the self from the body and the survival of selfhood beyond death. Transplant technology and the prolongation of life also have implications for the doctrine of man, and Christian faith cannot ignore these in developing its own anthropology or in shaping its proclamation.

The "Secularization" of Man

Christian faith has always assumed that man could not live without an ultimate, that if he did not worship the true God he would create a god for himself, that he would worship a graven image, wealth, and power, or even himself. Man's idols were pointed to as evidence that he is incurably religious. It was assumed that he could not live fully and meaningfully unless the short-term goals of his existence were made complete in the long-term meanings of God. Thus man was called by the theologians, *"homo religiosus"*—religious man—and our theology and preaching always assumed that this was a right description. Indeed, to call theology "answering theology" is to confess that our need for God and for the eternal is incurable. "Thou hast made us for thyself," said Augustine, "and we do not rest until we rest in thee."

Perhaps the most troubling fact of the modern world is the growing evidence that many men do indeed seem to get along without any conscious awareness of God. They do so "very well at that," said Dietrich Bonhoeffer, the German theologian murdered by the Hitler regime. There have always been those who took no thought of their souls, but in our day there seems to be reason to suspect such people are becoming the rule rather than the exception. The greatest challenge to traditional faith today is not the militant atheist but the serene secularist, the man who lives a whole and essentially healthy existence but feels no need for God. How do you address the gospel to him who feels no need, and asks no questions which cannot be adequately answered at the human level? What, indeed, if man is not after all incurably religious? What need does he have of God? Or is secular man deceiving himself? Is secularism the wave of the future, a permanent achievement and maturity of mankind? Then what is God to us? Is it a new expression of sin, a neurosis? How then do we expose it for what it is?

In all aspects of the modern world the same challenge is reflected to the contemporary Christian who is seeking to understand himself and his fellow-man in the light of his faith. To be a theologian in the best sense today is to live in the tension between traditional anthropology, the contemporary situation, and our participation in human existence as men of faith.

SUGGESTIONS FOR THOUGHT
AND DISCUSSION

1. It has been said that all the basic questions of our day are anthropological, that is, questions about man. Can you suggest ways in which modern life has threatened man's sense of value and his identity? How do such things as war, cybernetics and computer technology, space exploration, organ

transplants, evolution, development of the mass media of communication, ecological questions, etc., affect our understanding of what it is to be man?

2. Some have said that man doesn't really ask ultimate (religious) questions about himself any more. Is this true of the people you live and work with? If not, what sort of expression do such questions take?

3. The problematic character of human life usually confronts us in the midst of life. In what kind of situation is it apt to arise for you? Describe one such experience and try to put clearly the underlying questions. How might your faith speak to or answer these questions?

4. To what extent do you think the preaching you hear and the church literature you read are speaking to the real questions modern men are asking?

5. Discuss the "polar" nature of man. (See p. 142 f.) Is this a good description of your experience of being a person? Can you describe situations in which this polar nature became evident to you?

6. Consider the basic affirmations of the Christian doctrine of creation (pp. 150–52). Does contemporary man have difficulty with any of these affirmations? Which ones? Why?

7. It is said that modern man has no sense of sin. Do you think this is so? If not, what forms does such a sense take today? How can we shape our witness to speak to man's need as he experiences it?

CHAPTER NINE

Understanding God
(Theology Proper)

THE DOCTRINE OF GOD is the focal point of theology. This is
true both in a general sense for every age and in a special
sense for our day. In a general sense it is that to which the
doctrine of man points, as the answer to the questions raised
by our experience as men. In a special sense it is the central
religious problem for men in the late twentieth century.
While men in previous centuries have wrestled with other
questions of faith—sin and forgiveness, Christology, the authority of church and Scripture—it was usually on the basis
of a common assumption of the reality of God. It was not
God who was in question, but some particular understanding
of his self-revelation or of his way of working with men. The
dominant theology of the first half of the century, from
Barth to Tillich, shows a growing concern with the problem
of speaking meaningfully about God to contemporary man.
And the development of an essentially secular culture—one
which for the first time in Christian history feels competent
to deal with life without reference to eternal realities—has
created a challenge for the believer perhaps unequaled.
How does one speak of God—how does one become a "theo-

logian"—in such a world? The fact of secularism and the difficulty of speaking of God in clearly meaningful terms has given birth in recent years to a movement—variously called Christian Atheism, Radical Theology and "Theology of the Death of God"—which is committed to being Christian and to doing theology without God.

Can one be a theologian or a Christian without God? Not, certainly, if these words are to have meaning even remotely akin to their usual meaning. But the obvious depth of these men's commitment to try is a clue to the seriousness of the challenge to the Christian today. Contemporary men seem to have greater difficulty in grasping the traditional doctrine of God because they seem to find it difficult to *experience* God, at least in ways that make easy contact with Christian theology. Our task as Christian theologians is to learn to understand our neighbor's dilemma so that we can discover new and effective ways to communicate the reality of God to him. Furthermore, since Christians are modern men too, we also are troubled by the conflicts and contradictions of life and faith, so that our attempt to understand God is also the attempt to answer our own questions and to ground our own faith anew in him. Understanding God is necessary not just for purposes of persuasion, but of survival as men of faith. The question for many of us today is, in Paul van Buren's words, "How can I, who am a modern man, also be a Christian?"

THE TRADITIONAL MEANING OF GOD

Our wisdom, insofar as it ought to be deemed true and solid wisdom, consists almost entirely of two parts: the knowledge of God and of ourselves. But as these are connected together by many ties, it is not easy to determine which of the two precedes, and gives birth to the other. For in the first place, no man can survey himself without forthwith turning his thoughts toward God in whom he lives and moves. . . . On the other hand, it is evident that man never attains to a true self-knowledge until he has previously contemplated the face of God.

So spoke John Calvin in the opening paragraphs of his *Institutes of the Christian Religion*. The knowledge of man and the knowledge of God are correlates; they cannot be separated. This is reflected in all that we have said above. Man is the question, God is the answer, and nothing meaningful can be said about God which is not, directly or indirectly, meaningful to man *as man*.

This understanding explains why we have looked first at the doctrine of man. Not that man determines God, or that God is not in himself what he is, apart from what man thinks of him. It is simply that we do not know God except as he *comes to us* in our experience and in our world. Thus, as Luther clearly knew, God can never be more than an abstract conception of doubtful religious value except as he is received through the needs of our existence. God can never be *God* for me unless he is God *for me*.

This has always been the case in the biblical and also the specifically Christian doctrine of God. To be sure, the understanding of God changed, matured, and took on different shades of meaning through the Old and New Testaments. The same has been true throughout the history of doctrine as well. But every shift of understanding reflects some modification of the human situation and some new expression of human need. Now, it often happens that the real religious meaning of the doctrine of God—which is its meaning for men in need—is obscured by the formal theological expression which is given to it in creeds and dogma, especially when the passing of time allows the loss of the religious situation which gave birth to such creeds. It becomes the theologian's task to rediscover that religious meaning as the first step in giving it more contemporary and therefore more compelling expression.

God as Trinity—the Heart
of the Doctrine

Anyone who is familiar with the history of religion in general is aware of the many points of contact between the Christian doctrine of God and the understanding of God in other religions. Indeed, these similarities bear witness to the universality of the experience of worship and also to the common core of human need of which we have spoken. The church has not hesitated to make use of these points of contact in missionary activity. But is there any element of the Christian doctrine of God which is sufficiently unique to constitute a distinctly Christian content? If there is such, it is probably the Christian confession that the one God of faith exists and reveals himself in three persons—as Father, as Son and as Holy Spirit. Although this is by no means the least difficult of Christian affirmations, and has indeed caused perhaps as much agony of understanding among the elect as it has difficulty for the unbeliever, it has remained central to Christian faith. The doctrine of the Trinity has generally served to distinguish Christianity, at least formally, from its parent faith, Judaism. Judaic faith has remained committed to the "Shema" ("Hear, O Israel, the Lord is *one!*") as its central confession. And while, as we shall point out below, the difference in *substance* is not always clear, the doctrine of the Trinity has nevertheless been a stumbling block between many a Jew and the Christian faith.

My own experience suggests that there are few elements of Christian theology today which are more meaningless to the layman than the doctrine of the Trinity. The idea that "three is one and one is three," as one layman put it to me, is not only absurd but religiously meaningless; and more than a few intelligent Christians have relegated it to that special file of concepts to which they pay lip service but no longer seriously believe. Is the doctrine of the Trinity an essential part of Christian faith or is it merely baggage brought into our day from the misty metaphysics of the past?

Theologians themselves have not always agreed on an answer. Friedrich Schleiermacher, the "father" of contemporary theology, had serious doubts about the religious value of the Trinity for modern man. Schleiermacher was the first theologian to attempt a major reinterpretation of Christian theology for the modern world. He did so with great sympathy for traditional faith, and found meaning and value in most of the great doctrines of the past. Yet so little did the doctrine of the Trinity mean to him that he dealt with it rather negatively in an appendix to his great work, *The Christian Faith*. And through much of nineteenth and early twentieth century theology the trinitarian understanding of God was dealt with as an embarrassing necessity. However, the situation has changed significantly since then. One of the interesting characteristics of much post-liberal theology has been the rediscovery of the Trinity. Karl Barth's great dogmatics is trinitarian in its structure. Even more significant is the fact that Paul Tillich, whose theology has been more profoundly shaped by Schleiermacher than any other major theologian of our day, has returned to the trinitarian principle as the *basis* for his *Systematic Theology*.

Now, it is possible to deduce too much from this "rediscovery of the Trinity." The difficulties of the traditional doctrine are, if anything, greater today than they have been in the past. It does indicate, however, that a Christian theology without the triune God got itself into difficulties which seemed to demand his return. So faith has in recent years asked afresh about the meaning of this dogma. It seems clear that the formulation of the doctrine, with all of its verbal and logical difficulties, represented the church's attempt to give expression to something essential in its faith. What does the Trinity seek to say about God?

The doctrine of the Trinity is not, strictly speaking, a biblical doctrine. There is in the New Testament all the raw material necessary for the creation of such a doctrine, but it was not fully synthesized and given dogmatic status for about five centuries. Even less is there a clearcut doctrine of the Trinity in the Old Testament, although certain elements in the Hebrew concept of God clearly point in the direction of such a doctrine. One way of understanding the Trinity is to see it as the affirmation that God is a "living God." The Hebrew faith in its most mature state rejected any view of God which isolated him from active and providential control of his world and of the lives of his people. Yahweh was the God who had made himself known in the Exodus as the sovereign creator who directs the forces of nature and the events of history for his redemptive purposes. By confessing that God was a living God they affirmed that he was personal, active and purposive.

There are real difficulties for modern man in affirming that God is personal, and especially that he is "a person" among the persons of creation. Much of the difficulty of theism arises from the rather absurd and naïve expression which biblical personalism sometimes takes. We have become very much aware of the distortions which can be created by an uncritical anthropomorphism. In fact, the Hebrews themselves were aware of this danger and constantly warned against making God into man's alter ego. But they nevertheless understood that the meaning of human history hinged upon the fact that the power at the heart of the universe is neither indifferent to human values nor incapable of helping men in actualizing these values. The confession that God is living God is the Hebrew way of asserting that human history and value are affirmed by God himself. It may certainly be possible to modify and correct a naïve concept of God as living God, but it seems doubtful that the essential content of this doctrine can be surrendered without also surrendering the central affirmation that creation is good and that human life has meaning.

How does the doctrine of the Trinity express the idea of the living God? It does so by denying on the one hand that

God is a bare, empty unity (a transcendent without division or quality, as in monism). Such a being could never enter into relation with the men in a real world or love them. Nor is God on the other hand a plurality of forces, as in polytheism. Such a view of deity could never give unity to life and purpose to history. The living God is neither empty unity nor a chaotic play of cosmic forces. Rather, he is the being who possesses unity in diversity. And isn't unity in diversity the distinguishing quality of living reality? A being which has life is one which is constantly going out from self in a multitude of ways and returning to self by creating out of its experience a new living unity. This happens, for example, whenever I sit down at the dinner table. I take into me that which is not me and by the miracle of metabolism I unite it with myself. I do this also in every social event and relation. If I am vitally alive, every experience, every encounter with others calls me out from myself, causes me to interact creatively with the other, and results finally in a new self-integration in which I am still myself, yet larger and richer by that which has been added. Thus the "living God" is the triune God, who goes out from himself in creation to call into being over against himself a world, and then draws that world *back* to himself in the richer unity of reconciliation. Thus the idea of Trinity is not a matter of "three is one and one is three" at all, but it is an affirmation that God is not frozen in the death of abstraction. Rather he is the creating and creative *power* of being.

What we have been saying is that the deepest, most original source of the doctrine of the triune God is this sense of the living and redemptive concern and care of God. Yet the formal doctrine of the Trinity says more than this. It affirms specifically that God is manifest in three distinct forms or "persons." He is God the Father, God the Son (manifest in some form in Jesus Christ) and God the Holy Spirit. The problem of the meaning of person and the difficulty of conceiving the distinctions in the Godhead are now so be-

mired in centuries of controversy as to defy any clear solution. And it is not our purpose—perhaps not even our desire
—to clarify the clouded atmosphere of the trinitarian controversies. If the doctrine of the Trinity is to be meaningful
and usable again it must be because we recognize that it says
something essential about God, something which we also
must say if we will do justice to our own faith, whether we
use the old formulas or not. But what did these ancient formulas seek to say?

If we go back to the beginnings of the formal doctrine of the
Trinity in the first centuries of Christian history we find that
the church was aware of the reality of God in three rather
decisive manifestations, each of which was essential to their
confession of life and hope in him. They felt that they had
experienced the reality of God in three different activities or
modes, and these are the basis of all trinitarian thought. Indeed, the Trinity was the attempt to describe this threefold
encounter with God. As God the Father, God was creator and the source of all being. As God the Son, he was the
redeemer who entered history for their salvation. As God the
Spirit, he was the ever-present reality in the midst of life sanctifying it and making it whole. When the church spoke of
God as trinity it affirmed that he was creator, redeemer and
sanctifier. In insisting that these three are one—that is, three
modes of being or activity of the *one* god—they affirmed their
basic monotheism, established their genuine continuity with
Hebrew faith, and affirmed also the oneness of all of life under him. Unlike polytheism, with its breaking up of life into
warring forces—gods of the seas, of the heavens, gods of the
underworld—and unlike the dualism of the Gnostics of the
first century, who taught that creation came from the hand of
an evil God and was only partially redeemable—Christianity affirmed that creation, history and hope were all of a piece,
unified by the one creating, redeeming and sanctifying God.

Understood in this sense, the Trinity appears as the answer of the early church to the questions of existence which

confronted man in the living of life. The doctrine of the Trinity was "answering theology" in the finest tradition of the
church. Let us look more closely at the affirmations it contains, since it is likely that they must find some kind of expression in any adequate contemporary doctrine of God.

1. *Chaos, nothingness, and the Father.* In Genesis 1 God
calls the earth out of chaotic nothingness into the reality of
existence. "And the earth was without form and void . . .
and God said, let there be light!" In both the Old and New
Testaments, it is repeatedly affirmed that God not only origi-
nates the ordered world but that he continually sustains it in
existence. Now, it is important to remember that this confession is not merely cosmic but personal. It reflects the fact that
human life is lived at every moment on the edge of chaos and
of nothingness. We have no power of being in ourselves. We
have life, as it were, given to us, and our hold upon it is tenuous and fragile in the extreme. If there is even for a little
while order in chaos, vitality in the midst of universal entropy,
life in death, it depends upon the sufferance of God. "He
takes our breath away; we vanish into dust." Our hope that
life and love will not vanish in the absurdity of a meaningless
universe depends on the power at the heart of that universe.

What do we discover at the heart of life and of the world?
Faith confesses that we do not find chaos and death, but a
God who creates and calls it good! As we have seen, the affirmation of goodness, in reference to the universe as well as
to man, is a judgment about the future, about human hopes
and expectations. The confession that God is father affirms that the full range of universal history aims not at
chaos but at meaning. God as father is the sovereign God.
He is in control. He is providential God.

Now, the doctrine of divine providence, which is intimately
related to the doctrine of God as creator, has been a troublesome doctrine in Christian history, since it has often been
understood to be equivalent to divine determinism. In traditional Calvinism, for example, the sovereignty of God was

understood to be so complete as to amount to total divine causation in the most minute event of the universe. Such a view does violence to the human experience of freedom and of responsibility. Many modern people have justly reacted against such an all-consuming understanding of deity. One does not glorify God by reducing man to the level of an automaton. Thus the way in which the sovereignty of God manifests itself, and how that sovereignty can be expressed without doing violence to human freedom, needs to be carefully rethought in our century. But the affirmation that God is providential father would seem to be the foundation of everything else that the Christian can say about him.

2. *Disruption, sin and the Son.* God is not only the answer to the question of our finitude, he is also the answer to the question of our sin. Our lives are disrupted, and disordered, we are alienated from ourselves, from each other and from God. We need to know not only that we are given being by God but that we are also accepted by him and reconciled. The redemptive nature of God which is implied in the doctrine of creation has been made explicit in the Son. In Jesus Christ the believer is made aware in a decisive and never-to-be surpassed way that God is not only power; he is also love. To be told that God is creative power, that he is the ground of our being, even that he is good remains of doubtful value in itself. Divine goodness can become the very thing which threatens to destroy us, because we know that we are not good. His goodness becomes a barrier; his holiness only deepens our anguish. In the Son we discover God the redeemer, whose goodness manifests itself through reconciliation and atonement. God the Father sustains us in *being.* In God the Son we come to know that he also sustains us in love.

3. *Loneliness and the Spirit.* The doctrine of the Holy Spirit was longer in achieving theological structure than were the other expressions of the Trinity, even though the Spirit plays a central part in the New Testament itself. It is also probable that the concept of the Spirit remains amorphous

and difficult for many Christians today. Indeed, I know many basically conservative theologians who will in private confess that they don't quite know what to make of the doctrine. Part of the difficulty lies in the contemporary problem with the idea of "spirit" in general. What does one understand by a distinct personal reality who manifests himself in disembodied form? And how much more disturbing is the employment, usually in hymns or liturgy, of the archaic expression "Holy Ghost." Furthermore, many Christians have difficulty in distinguishing the activity of the Spirit from that of God himself and from that of Christ, especially since it is usually affirmed that each is active in the other, and since the New Testament itself can frequently use Holy Spirit, Spirit of God, and Spirit of Christ interchangeably. What does the Holy Spirit add to a doctrine of God? Our concern here is once again not to untangle the difficulties described, but to discover what the church was saying at the Council of Constantinople in 381 when it affirmed that the Spirit was "with Father and Son . . . worshipped and glorified together." Why did the church come increasingly to attribute to the Holy Spirit the full dignity of God?

The answer lies in the fact that the Holy Spirit represented the direct and living presence of God then and there in the midst of their lives. To the question "Where do we meet God?" the answer had to be not twofold but threefold. As creator he is in all places and all times, but his presence is only felt indirectly, through the world. As redeemer, he was first met in Jesus, but after the ascension Jesus became a fact of the past. He was a historical event to which they looked back in thanksgiving and joy, but he was nonetheless past. But the church found that they also knew God in a third way, namely, as the life-giving presence with them every moment, sanctifying, reassuring and empowering. The doctrine of the Holy Spirit has been the church's way of affirming the "presence" of God in the lives of his people. It is he who unites the energies and the longings of the soul, making life one. It is he who fills the emptiness of life with the reassuring word, "Fear thou not, for I am with thee." Thus if the answer to the question of chaos and death is "God the Father," and the answer to the question of sin is "God the Son," then the answer to the question of the loneliness of life is "God the Spirit." And these are, so goes the confession, "one and the same" God.

How is the Christian today to understand the divine "persons" and relate them to his own doctrine? Is it possible to see them as "modes," or differing roles or functions of a single God, much as, let us say, a man might according to need function as father, husband, and friend? Many Christians, especially in the West, have tended to view them in this way. Such a way of understanding is usually called modalism, and was, in its extreme forms at least, declared to be a heresy by the ancient church. However, I suspect that since Augustine most Christians have conceived of one personal God who manifests himself in three modes of activity. Such a "functional" trinity runs the danger of losing the gospel only if it suggests that these "roles" are merely accidental or temporary, and that God as he really is remains hidden and mysterious to man. The heart of the Christian doctrine of God as Trinity is the confession that God has come out from behind the mask and at last can be known for what he is. He *really is* creator, he *really is* redeemer, he *really is* sanctifier and paraclete (the "one who walks beside"). And any attempt to reshape our understanding of God for our own day will need to somehow preserve the substance of this confession, whatever it does with the form. Otherwise we will have come close to the boundary which separates faith from unfaith.

THE PROBLEM OF GOD TODAY

More theological "muscle" is required today to understand the meaning of God in our own lives and to be able to ex-

press that meaning effectively than was true in the past. As
we have said above, the problems of belief in God are real for
the person who values integrity and wholeness and who wants
to look without self-deception at his world. This is why
responsible belief is always in tension with troubling doubt.
The more genuine and fundamental a Christian's faith, the
more determined he is to confront life with all of its disturbing reality, and to wrestle with the ambiguities of life in the
light of that faith. The faith which cannot confront challenge or wrestle with difficulty is a doubtful faith, and may
be a camouflage for fear. A maturing faith, which should be
one of the goals of theological understanding, is willing to
challenge its own most precious presuppositions because God
alone is truth. Thus it is well for the person who is seeking
to develop a mature doctrine of God to recognize the genuineness of the difficulties in the way of faith today. Only by
doing so will he be able to see the problems in their proper
perspective. Also, having hurt with other men in their doubt,
he will have the ability and the right to speak with them of
God.

The challenge to faith which we earlier called secularism
is too complex a thing to be dealt with briefly. We can mention only a few of the central difficulties which stand between
modern men and traditional faith. It is important for us to
understand that the basic problems are not merely intellectual.
They are apt to be deeply felt before they are ever consciously
thought about. This is why glib answers and clever arguments
do not make them go away. They are what my graduate
students call "gut issues." Thus the believer must live with
them and feel their ache before he can begin to be healed
himself and able to help others.

Do We Need God?

As we have seen, God in traditional faith is the answer to
the questions of life. Man becomes aware of God, said Til-

lich, in the "boundary-situations," when his own incompleteness and lack of self-sufficiency become clear. "Man's extrem-
ity," goes the pulpit cliché, "is God's opportunity." And in
past centuries the helplessness of man in a cosmos which
largely overwhelmed him equipped him psychologically for
God. Indeed, almost all Christian preaching and persuasion
was rooted in the conviction that man could not endure existence without God. Flood, famine and plague gave substance
to the church's *memento mori*. In the last two centuries this
situation has changed appreciably, and it does the believer no
good to insist that man is substantially as helpless as he ever
was. He doesn't *feel* helpless. He has made spectacular progress in controlling the forces of nature which formerly reduced
him to terror. He has found answers to problems which have
plagued men since history began. Furthermore, the brevity
and drabness of life which made it easy for the medieval man
to look for fulfillment beyond life have vanished. Whatever
modern life is, it is not dull; and it is, at least for most of
us much of the time, a life of interest, challenge and excitement. Medical and technological science hold forth the
promise of removing even the threat of death, or of post-
poning it to such a distance that it no longer alarms us.

Now, the point in all this progress is not that man has
risen above problems. Indeed, with almost every advance new
problems arise; for instance, the conquest of disease leads to
a population explosion. The point is that most really modern
men no longer feel that they need God to solve their problems
or to hold their hands. They are convinced that most of
their difficulties can be solved by human means, and they
seem willing for the most part to live with those that remain. Such self-sufficiency may be evil or good, or both. Some
see it as the final stage of the fall—the attempt of man to become his own God—and therefore the purest expression of
his rebellion and sin. Others see it as, in some respects at
least, a wholesome development; for example, they point to
it as evidence of a new maturity in which man accepts the

responsibility of the image of God. Dietrich Bonhoeffer saw this new sufficiency as man's "coming of age," and suspected that God himself was behind it, like a loving father who must more and more let the son taste the freedom and responsibility of manhood. But the point in either case is, if we do not feel a need for God, how can we understand him? What place does he take? What role does he play in our lives? And how do we speak of God to men who get along very well on their own? Once it was argued that men could not live by short-term goals, values and meanings, and that these short-term goals had to be given significance by participating in the ultimate or eternal purposes of God. But what do you say to make eternal matters urgent to a man who seems to be fulfilled and happy with his day-by-day involvement in human endeavors—especially when in all honesty he seems to be as healthy and integrated as those who are obsessed by the eternal? Who and what is God to the man who can get along without him?

Can We Know God?

Perhaps even more troubling than the self-sufficiency of man is the difficulty modern men have in experiencing God or in finding a "place" for him. This means first a place in the universe. Ancient man conceived of the world as a limited physical environment bounded by other spheres and finally by heaven. Heaven was a specific and conceivable place which was the dwelling place of God. Even today most of our uncritical thoughts place God "up there" someplace, and much of the biblical imagery reflects this, for example, the ascension of Christ up into the clouds. This two-level universe pointed to a basic truth, that God must somehow transcend the limits of our world and its natural order if he is to have meaning for us as God. The doctrine of divine transcendence affirms that God is not "caught" in the dilemmas and ambiguities of life in the world.

But we no longer live in a two-level universe. On the contrary, for contemporary men there is one cosmos—a *universe*—and however many surprises the universe may hold, however many undiscovered galaxies and planets lie beyond our purview, we assume that whatever is is a part of *this* sphere, and subject to the laws and the conditions of existence incumbent on the known world. Modern men have difficulty conceiving of a transcendent sphere where the laws and limits of this universe do not apply. Where then *is* God? The question can take silly forms but it is *not* a silly question. Can any of us seriously entertain the suggestion of Jonathan Edwards that heaven or hell must be on distant planets within our universe? One reason that John A. T. Robinson's little book *Honest to God* made such an impact on lay readers a few years ago is that he forthrightly and honestly confessed that for him the God "up there" had ceased to be. Many readers will realize that it was so for them too.

Not only has God been crowded out of the world spatially, but he has also to a great extent been banished functionally. In the past God has often seemed evident in the gaps in man's knowledge and ability. That which man could not understand was the prerogative of God, and what he could not produce or control seemed necessarily the product of God's activity. The origin and abatement of a plague, the sending or withholding of the rain, the creation of life . . . here man's limit left room for and seemed to require God. Does drouth wither the crops? It is God's judgment! Does the rain come and refresh the land? It is God's bounty! Little by little, however, this "God of the gaps" has been crowded out of nature by the increase of man's technical knowledge and prowess. If viruses cause plagues and air masses determine the rain, where do we confront God? Theology has all too often fought a rear-guard action, trying to hold on to the gaps that remained only to see them one by one close upon us. Probably the last remaining gap has been closed by the recent synthesis of living organisms from inert matter in the laboratory.

Again the point is not whether answers can be given to the problems implied by this situation. The point is the impact it has made on man's spirit. I suspect that the sense of the reality of any transcendent realm or being has been all but smothered in many people today by the "blanket of nature." Where in the world do we meet God?

One answer to this question has been "in the human soul." Ever since God began to disappear from nature, believers have sought to validate God and faith by the appeal to inner, religious experience. Not "out there," but "in here"! In fact, both liberalism, which appealed to religious experience, and neoorthodoxy, which stressed the I-thou encounter with God, turned to internal evidence. We know God, it is said, not by proofs based on nature but by the witness of our hearts. Faith is "self-validating." One knows it by the "deep stirring of the soul." And while this approach is still powerful and meaningful, even the appeal to inwardness has its difficulties. As depth psychology and neurology progress, we are learning more about the physiological and psychological causes of personality and of personal experience. What if that "deep stirring of the soul" turns out to be a restive ulcer or a message from our own id, rather than the Word of God? How are we to distinguish between a traumatic hallucination and an encounter with the Divine? And what if we don't have encounters? There seems to be some evidence that contemporary people are having real difficulties in this area. If we peg our case for God on the encounter and it doesn't come, where do we turn for God?

Can We Believe in God?

Perhaps the most penetrating problem for the thinking person, including the Christian, is the problem of tragedy and evil. In the past the church has often argued for God on the basis of the order of the universe. But what of the disorder and chaos? What does this say of God? There has always been suffering, but no century has seen more human agony than this one, or seen it so clearly. Bloodshed, hunger, hatred and fear have been brought home to us with unparalleled impact by the flourishing of the mass media of communication. The legacy of Hiroshima and Auschwitz has been for many the death of God. As for myself, if there are moments when I stand on the brink of unbelief, it is those moments when I contemplate the horror and agony which I see written so often on the face of man.

The effort of the Christian to understand and interpret the fact of evil in the light of faith is called *theodicy*, which means literally the "justification of God." At the heart of the problem of theodicy are the two central affirmations of Christian theology, God's sovereignty and his love. The problem of evil asks how both can be true. How could a good God allow the burning of Dresden or the agony of starvation in Biafra? If he is good, how can he be in control? If he is in control, how can he be good? The Christian's ability to deal meaningfully with this problem and to make the message of the gospel real amid the suffering of the world will have a bearing on the future of faith in that world.

There are, of course, other problems which are a part of the theological situation—the problem of finding images and language which communicate to an urban culture what the pastoral images of other centuries did for their day. The question of how human language can be used meaningfully to talk about the mystery of God is a related one. But most of the basic problems for a Christian doctrine of God center finally in the loss of the sense of the transcendent of which we have spoken above.

RETHINKING OUR UNDERSTANDING
OF GOD

What is the Christian to make of the situation? He must take the problems with full seriousness and try to understand them without blinking, but he must also take seriously the resources of his own faith and of the church. He must strive again to be both contemporary and Christian. Certainly the situation calls for an honest and frank reevaluation of our understanding of God. It has been said that much of the problem lies not in God's reality or in his ability to manifest himself, but in the inadequacy of traditional descriptions of God. And it is probably true that many of the images or ideas which hover around the name "God" are no longer adequate to their intention. Some of them aren't even biblical. Ideas which serve in one period of history or which for the individual are adequate at one stage of life may not be adequate for another period or stage. Men may be right in being uncomfortable with God-talk which has been outgrown or is contradictory. Many of our traditional concepts, though they grow out of a genuine religious purpose, may need revising or even replacing. For example, the naïve image of God in a spatial heaven cannot work today for most people. His transcendence has to be more than spatial or it is nothing at all. The custom of thinking of God as the "cosmic bellhop" who exists to serve as our problem solver rather than to receive our worship and praise certainly needs to be rethought. Although there is truth in this view, it demeans God and justifies the accusation made by Feuerbach and Freud that he is the projection of our wishes. We must also seek to better understand how God can be God in a world where man must assume his own responsibility—where man has come of age.

One aspect of traditional theology which is undergoing examination today is the concept of the absoluteness of God. The biblical meaning of God's absoluteness is that in him the ambiguities of finite life do not apply. He is above the threat of death, nonbeing and evil which are our lot in time. However, in Christian history this biblical meaning came to be combined with the Greek philosophical understanding, according to which the Divine is the absolute which transcends all concrete limitations. Such a God could have no determinate quality whatsoever. He (it?) was "pure being," since he had no potentiality at all. He could not change, for perfection would have to change to imperfection, it was said, nor could he have any real relations at all, for such would compromise his perfect self-sufficiency. For such a god, time is not real, since temporality is the stuff of finitude.

On the surface it seemed to the fathers of the medieval period that these two understandings of God's perfection—the religious and the philosophical—were the same. But many a Christian has wondered about a theology which spoke of an unchangeable God and of the living God in the same breath. Much of the theological weariness of the age may come from a doctrine of God which at its heart is contradictory. I remember when I was a boy being puzzled by a teacher who told me of God's love and his understanding, and then insisted to me that God did not understand as we do, but knew all in an instant, since time was not real for God. How could this be? What can it mean to say that God cannot be related to me, that he cannot change from his absolute perfection, that time is not real for God when love, understanding and historical activity are inseparably bound up with the real stuff of life and time? If God has acted in history, then history and time must be real for God. Many practical difficulties in Christian faith and life can be traced to a definition of transcendence or perfection which puts God out of touch with humanity and its world. Similarly, our attempts to do justice to God's power and sovereignty have often led us to describe his providential activity in terms of a thoroughgoing divine determinism. The religious doctrine of God's all-sufficient control is not the same thing as a deterministic predestination. A God too absolute in power can be a threat to human responsibility and freedom, since his determination of all events in nature and history reduces human creativity to nothing and violates one of the deepest affirmations of experience. However God's perfection is understood, it must do justice to the biblical living God who achieves his purpose in dynamic and loving relationship with man.

In an interesting way modern man may be in a better position to take seriously the idea of the living God than were men of past centuries. Until about 1800 the generally accepted world view was a static, essentially unchanging one. As we have seen, however, the world of modern man is a living world, a world in process. In all the sciences, physics included, the basic facts are not things any more but *events*, not stuff but energy. The dominant feeling of our world is change. We are in movement, and our children's world will not be our world, nor will tomorrow be today. The philosophy of the present tends to reflect this dynamic view of life, as, for example, the so-called process philosophies of men such as John Dewey, Henri Bergson and A. N. Whitehead. Many theologians have seen this dynamic view of reality as opening up the possibility for meaningful God-talk today. If a static absolute cannot be a God for a world in process, perhaps a process God—a living God for a living world—can make God real anew.

What finally must a Christian understanding of God preserve? What are the essentials? I wonder if the whole affair cannot be summarized in two terms. One could call them transcendence and immanence, but these are technical terms. We can express the religious heart of the matter more simply. He must be sovereign, that is, sufficiently in control to give direction to life and history. And he must be love. If he is not love, he is not God, and human values become lost in a hostile world. If he is not sovereign, his love is sentimental and finally pointless, for he cannot give those human values their hope of permanence. The Christian God is both sovereign (and provident) and love. Or better yet, he is "sovereign love."

SUGGESTIONS FOR THOUGHT AND DISCUSSION

1. Write down on paper or blackboard several statements about God as you understand him. Are there any of the statements which appear to disagree or conflict? Discuss.

2. Do you think of God as a person? Are there problems with so describing God? How essential is the idea of person-hood in God for your faith? Is it helpful to speak of God as "personal" rather than as *a* person?

3. Have three members of your group discuss the question of God's omniscience (perfect knowledge), his omnipotence (perfect power) and prayer. (If God is all-knowing and all-powerful, what good does it do to pray?)

4. How important is the doctrine of the Trinity to your theology? If you were asked to provide an illustration or analogy to explain the Trinity, what would it be? Analyze each other's contributions.

5. What "person" of the Trinity—Father, Son or Holy Spirit—is most real to you, or most understandable? Which is most difficult or least real? Why? What do these imply about your understanding of God? What do they imply about the way in which you feel need?

6. Can men live healthy and whole lives without refer-ence to God? Don't answer hastily. Reread pp. 71–73 and then think about your friends and acquaintances.

CHAPTER TEN

Understanding Christ
(Christology)

WE HAVE SEEN in the previous chapter that the doctrine of God is the beginning and the end of theology. But we have also said that for the Christian the fundamental question, "What is God like?" is answered in Jesus the Christ. The Christian faith is most readily distinguished from other religions with which it shares much—Judaism, for instance—by the crucial role which Jesus plays, not just historically, but religiously as well. To be a Christian in more than a cultural sense is to refer all of one's life and faith back to Jesus the founder. Any theology, personal or otherwise, in which Christ plays a marginal or incidental role must be suspect from the beginning.

This does not mean, however, that any particular understanding of Christ, his person, his role in reconciliation or redemption, or his value for the Christian life, has held exclusive sway in Christian history. There has probably been a wider range of opinion in Christology than has been the case with regard to the doctrine of man or of God. In fact, controversy over the christological question became so intense in the first four centuries of Christian history that it threatened to tear the church asunder—and the Roman Empire as well. Out of this controversy came the first attempt of the church, by means of theological councils, to establish a theological norm for the definition of Christian faith. In a series of conciliar decisions climaxing in the Council of Chalcedon in A.D. 451, the traditional formula for understanding Christ was hammered out. It is usually referred to as the *two-natures doctrine*. This formula by no means answered all the questions which could be raised concerning Christ's place in the Christian faith. In fact, it said rather little about the actual nature of Christ except negatively, that is, by ruling out christological opinions which were felt to violate the essence of faith in him. Therefore what Chalcedon did was to set out the *limits* of Christology. Beyond these one could not go without falling into heresy. It also as a result set out a broad range between these limits within which theology could explore the meaning of Christ.

It is interesting to note that the Chalcedonian formula has had on the whole a unifying influence on Christian history, so that most of the really divisive controversies since 451 have tended to be on other questions than the christological one. Whatever its limitations, it apparently gave sufficiently clear expression to the essential insights of belief in Christ and sufficient latitude for individual difference to enfold many different species of Christian thought. Even during the Reformation period, when Christendom was split between three warring camps—Roman, Reform, and Anabaptist (or Sectarian)—all three on the whole gave allegiance to and defended the adequacy of the doctrine of the two natures. And even in modern times, when the christological problem has asserted itself anew and many critics of Chalcedon have arisen, it still remains the heart of most official church confessions.

What does Chalcedon say? It seeks to affirm the full and complete humanity of Christ while also affirming his true and full divinity. It also insists that these two natures, divine and human, are manifest in a complete unity of person. Christ is one Lord and Savior, yet fully human and fully divine. This "two natures in one" quality is expressed in all the decisive phrases of the formula of Chalcedon. Christ is acknowledged as being

> . . . one and the same Son, our Lord Jesus Christ, at once complete in Godhead and complete in manhood, truly God and truly man, . . . of one substance with the Father as regards his Godhead, and at the same time of one substance with us as regards his manhood. . . . As regards his Godhead, begotten of the Father before all ages, but yet as regards his manhood, begotten for us men and for our salvation, of Mary the Virgin . . . ; one and the same Christ, Son, Lord, only begotten, recognized in two natures, without confusion, without change, without division, without separation. . . .

But what does Chalcedon mean? Assuming that the fathers of the fifth century understood what *they* meant by these phrases which they wove together in a not-always-too-transparent way, what can they mean to us today? What can two natures in one person mean? Can a modern mind resolve the paradoxes of this formula? The phrases seem to struggle together, like Jacob and Esau in the womb. It may have been possible to obscure the logical absurdity of the language while a philosophy of substance still prevailed, but in our day this possibility doubtless no longer exists. It was Schleiermacher who pointed out that nothing—not even God—could properly be said to have *two* natures, since the word nature means *what a thing is*. An entity could have two or more aspects to its *one* nature—it could logically, if not conceivably, be half divine and half human—or it could be two natures and therefore two *beings*—but not two natures in one. Not even the threeness-in-one of the Trinity presents us with the verbal difficulties we find in the twoness-in-one of Chalcedon. How can we make sense out of this central confession of the church which, it has been said, is "believed by all and understood by none"?

In Part 1 of this study we discussed the question of the lay theologian's attitude toward the past, especially in reference to the problem of creedalism and anticreedalism. We observed that the proper stance might be a kind of "reverent disrespect." Such an attitude would feel in no sense bound to the formulas of the past, yet it would seek to preserve their power and value even while questioning their form. Indeed, our desire to preserve their value requires that we undertake the task of correcting and translating them according to the demands of faith today. Perhaps such an approach can prove helpful in understanding the meaning of Chalcedon for the believer of the present.

GETTING BEHIND CHALCEDON

Where Did Christology Begin?

It is important for us to remember that all creeds, however hard they work at being final definitions, are at heart confessions. (The word *credo* means literally, "I believe.") And this is true of the church's great christological creeds. Though Chalcedon expresses itself in the language of Greek metaphysics, the heart of it is a believer's "credo." In other words, the two-natures doctrine did not come into existence because of a philosopher's curiosity about the nature of things. It came into being because the faith of the church struggled to express itself. Therefore, to be able to say what this doctrine means, we must examine the religious experience of the church which created it.

Where did Christology begin? Once again the answer has to be "at the beginning." That is, it grew out of the experience of the apostles with Jesus before his ascension and the experience of the church with the Holy Spirit after the ascension. As we have seen, there was no worked-out Christology in the New Testament period, but there was a series of experiences with Christ and there was a new reality called the church, all of which were loaded with christological implications. A host of feelings and unformed convictions with regard to Christ clamored for expression and gave birth to the earliest christological thought.

Now at this point an important distinction needs to be made. Traditionally, the doctrine of Christ has been divided into two related doctrines. It is customary to speak of the person and the work of Christ. The former seeks to answer concerning Christ the question, "Who was he (and who *is* he)?" The second speaks to the question, "What has he done for us?" Now it is evident that these two questions cannot be separated, but it makes a considerable difference in the tone of a person's theology which question he begins with. Most systematic treatments of Christology in the past have begun with the person of Christ, on the assumption —doubtless correct—that it was his unique quality or character which made possible his redemptive work. So also most of our popular thinking about Christ moves from person to work. "If he had not been God's son," it is said, "he couldn't have done what he did," namely, become our Savior. This understanding explains the passionate resistance of so many church members and pastors to anything which seems to belittle the full divinity of Christ, even when they are driven by this fear in the direction of docetism.

When we look at the two-natures doctrine, it seems also to deal primarily with the person of Christ—"two natures, one person, . . . complete in Godhead, manhood," etc. But if we dig more deeply into the controversies which led to Chalcedon, we begin to sense the concerns which are its real source, and these concerns are at heart occupied not so much with who or what he is, as with what he has *done*. One small phrase in the creed reveals the real religious motivation of all Christology, namely that he came "for us men and for our salvation." The heart of Christology lies in Christ's *work*, in what he has done for us.

Thus we are provided with a very important principle of interpretation and reconstruction. Whatever the *logical* order, (person to work?), the actual experience of the church has moved from work to person. The Apostolic church before Pentecost knew that their encounter with this man Jesus was decisive for them and for all men. They had the experienced fact of reconciliation, and a sense of a new reality in their midst. Their experience parallels that of the man born blind related in John 9. First came the opening of the eyes, then in halting steps came the conclusions about the Lord's identity ("A man called Jesus. . . . He is a prophet. . . . If he were not of God, he could do nothing. . . . Lord, I believe!"). In a similar halting way the church was led from what Christ had done in them to attributing to him the full and perfect dignity of God. We can best get behind Chalcedon by asking what the church was trying to express in its Christology. What is the religious experience hidden behind the formula? Then we will be in a position to think about our own Christology, for it also must finally be confessional. Like the early church, we also must ask, "What is Christ to us, and what does this imply concerning him?" In the light of our experience, what are we driven to include in our own credo?

The Heart of the Church's Faith

What was the content of the early church's experience with Christ? It varied from individual to individual, and that variation is reflected in the New Testament itself. To some he was a prophet in the line of the prophets, though immeasurably the greatest. To others he was the giver of a new law replacing and transcending the Law of Moses. To some he was a sacrifice unto God, atoning for their sins. There was little clarity and much variety of opinion in the first few years of the church. But gradually as the ground narrowed, particularly through the efforts of the two great theological giants of the New Testament, Paul and John, certain themes began to appear with increasing frequency. These themes probably emerged because they made contact with the experience of redemption that the church was seeking to express. Three such themes seem to stand out as the essence of what Christ had come to mean to the church:

1. *He was revealer.* They were convinced that Jesus was the fulfillment and completion of the prophetic line through which God had revealed himself to Israel. Yet they gradually came to see that he was an altogether unique revealer, not only in the clarity and completeness with which he manifested the Father but also in the credentials by which he did so. All previous revelation had had a fragmentary and broken character and was finally as much a concealing as a revealing. This was because the prophets were men, and their word was always filtered through the veil of their own imperfect understanding. This is why each prophet had to be superseded by another. The church sensed that while Christ functioned as a prophet he did so in a decisive and final way. He not only spoke for God; he confronted them with the *reality* of God. They could not imagine, after Jesus, that any more fundamental vision of God could be vouchsafed to them. Indeed, the one who had seen Jesus had seen the Father.

The revelatory work of Christ was twofold. First, it was a revelation of God's nature. In Jesus, the deep mystery of existence was finally and decisively answered. Even the greatest of the prophets left ambiguous the ultimate nature of reality and therefore left open the deepest questions of human existence. Christ pulled aside the veil and gave them a glimpse of God *as he was.* Or to use the language of John, he spoke with the very voice of God. Thus they came to refer to him as God's *logos,* his "word" or self-communication to men. And it may be that this motif of Christ as the final revelation underlies all the others and explains why the church has been so doggedly christocentric throughout its history. Why Christ? Because in him we have gotten a decisive glimpse into what reality is all about. He is the break in the mists of existence for the believer. To see God through Christ is to understand that no more basic vision is possible. In Christ we know the deepest secret of the Father; namely that he is love.

As final revelation, Christ revealed not only the essence of God—that he is love—but also something of his intent and purpose. In Christ, God's redemptive working in history and the final outcome of history became clear. In him they had been assured of their participation in the final victory of God and in the Kingdom to come.

2. *He was reconciler.* The church was not only convinced that Jesus had *revealed* God but that he had *reconciled* them to God. They were not only ignorant, they were also sinners, and Christ had spoken to them the word of reconciliation. But they sensed once again that he had done more than *announce* the acceptance of God—as one who having brought the word then becomes himself superfluous. In some way he was central both to the accomplishment of that reconciliation and to its continuing reality in the life of the redeemed. Somehow, reconciliation with God and participation in God's mercy were "in him."

The attempts of the New Testament church to understand how Christ's life and death were redemptive represent the beginning of a doctrine of the *atonement*, that branch of Christology that seeks to understand the role of Christ in bringing about reconciliation of man with God. In speaking of atonement, the church drew its language and concepts from a wide variety of sources, Hebrew and Greek, and passed down to later generations a vocabulary rich in imagery— the imagery of reconciliation, justification, sacrifice, propitiation, ransom, and satisfaction. But it is probably safe to say that no clear and consistent "theory" of the atonement emerged in the New Testament. In fact, the doctrine of the atonement has never received the kind of precise formulation that has been the case with the doctrine of God or the two-natures doctrine of Christ.

3. *He was giver of a new life.* In Christ the church not only came to know the truth of God and to be reconciled and forgiven through him; they also came to know deliverance from death and the beginning of a new life, a life which they could properly call eternal. Now, when the early church thought of reconciliation and atonement, they tended to think of the cross as the primary atoning event, and so cross and atonement represented one side of redemption. When they thought of the quality of newness experienced in him, of deliverance from the death of sin and victory over their own mortality, the resurrection became the key to their understanding. Christ was the one who had won the victory over death and in whose victory they shared. Just how much this assurance of victory over death meant to the Apostolic church is made clear by the fact that the resurrection became the heart of the early Christian preaching.

Thus the work of Christ as revealer, reconciler and giver of eternal life became the source of the early church's doctrine of Christ and drove them to attribute to him a dignity sufficient to make sense out of what he had done for them. And this order remains the probable order of procedure for every personal understanding of Christ in every age. We must ask first, "What has Christ done for us?" Having answered this question, we are prepared for the second question, "What must we therefore say of him?"

What we have said above puts us in a better position to understand the two-natures doctrine as the church's attempt to give expression to its experience of redemption in Christ. Therefore it is no more an attempt to argue the absurdity that two is one than the doctrine of the Trinity is an affirmation that three is one. It is rather an attempt to hold together in their understanding of Christ what they saw to be essential to redemption. Let us look at these affirmations more closely.

"Truly God and Truly Man"

He is "truly man. . . ." The joyful hope of the church lay in the conviction that God had entered into human experience. The Christian doctrine of *incarnation* (in-flesh-ing) is the rejection of the pessimism concerning the world and human life which had fixed itself upon the late Hellenic society. The gods had been driven by cultural collapse and social chaos into a limbo so remote that they seemed to disappear. For vast areas of Greco-Roman culture god was dead, or at least so remote that human existence was bereft of any direction, hope or goodness. Indeed, most of the philosophies and religions of this period were dualistic. This means that they sharply distinguished the sphere of the divine, which was transcendent, good and spiritual, from the physical order—that of the flesh, nature and history. The latter was considered to be worthless and evil. Is it any wonder that they became world-denying and ascetic, seeking to escape the corruption of corporeality and hoping to rise to the sphere of the divine?

Yet in this environment of contempt for the flesh these Christians proclaimed that God himself had actually become man! Their insistence that the Christ was not merely a theophany (an "appearance" of God, as in some of the Old Testament narratives) but truly and totally a man is the confession that in Jesus Christ God made clear his involvement in human history and life. Even as Jesus sanctified both wine and the wedding at Cana of Galilee, he comes as the sanctifying assurance that God is involved in human experience. It is not that God sends word to us as one would send a message from afar; he becomes *one with us*. The meaning of the true manhood of Christ can be summarized then by two affirmations: (1) History and nature are good! There is nothing inherently evil in the world or in flesh. Thus the Christian is able to affirm the essential goodness of his body, his world, and his history, and to see that these have lasting value even to God, because he did not hesitate to take *on our flesh*. (2) The universe cares about selves like us. The incarnation says that the world is real for God, and that he has involved himself in our life for our sake. The word of the gospel is, as Martin Luther saw, an assurance of "the humanity of God," expressed in his taking on humanity for our sakes. The involvement of God in our history and our flesh assures us that the power at the heart of the universe values selfhood and stands against any attempt, however well intended, to degrade man or to belittle his value or significance.

He is "truly God. . . ." If Chalcedon was firm in its insistence on the full reality of Jesus' manhood, it was even more emphatic that his humanity be allowed in *no* way to qualify his deity. The church had with each passing generation become more convinced that he was in some real sense God. In order to understand the value of Christ for faith and to do justice to his redemptive power, they felt they could say no less about him than this. Why did they feel that it was not enough to say that he was a good man, or even a prophet? The confession that Christ was "very God of very God" was the church's way of affirming the final adequacy of redemption in him. One who is only a man, even a very wise and a very good one, is still immersed in the ambiguity and the brokenness of life. Remember, man is the *question* of existence, not its answer. To insist that God was in Christ, or that Christ was God, is to insist that though he was imbedded in history as we, he was not and is not subject to the estrangement and emptiness of life as we know it.

In terms of revelation he was the unique and final light, because he alone had unbroken unity with God and could reveal to them the Father without refraction and distortion, incompleteness or tentativeness. He was the final word. There was nothing in God knowable by men or needed by them which had not been made manifest in Jesus. "He that hath seen me hath seen the Father," he told the disciples. The prophets, like good signposts, pointed beyond themselves. They said, "Lo, there!" Jesus said, "Here!" The church did not hope to go beyond him, but only to deepen what they had learned in him.

In terms of redemption, *truly God* meant that he shared the general sinfulness of life, but was not subject to it. He was "tempted as we," but was not under sin's power. He shared their anguish but not their helplessness. In Jesus the church had found one who was not a part of the problem but was its answer. They had met God not only as revealer but also as reconciler. He was "truly God."

In terms of victory over our mortality, truly God means that he shares the pain and anxiety which is the fruit of our finitude "even unto death," yet he does not share our helplessness in the face of pain and death. He sanctified our suffering in his cross and he overcame our mortality by his resurrection. He is "truly God," for in him the power of God as revealer, reconciler, and bringer of eternal life have decisively appeared.

There were those from the beginning who found it impossible to hold these two confessions together, or who for various reasons found it desirable to emphasize the one or the other side of the christological confession. Indeed, it is likely that most Christians have leaned in the direction of one or the other of the classical christological "heresies." One of these was Ebionism. *Ebionism* was the name given to the tendency to stress the real humanity of Christ as moral guide or prophetic preacher to the point of virtually excluding the divine. The opposite tendency, usually called *docetism*, resulted from placing such an exclusive emphasis on Christ's "godness" that his humanity was reduced to insignificance, or so transformed and infused by the power of God as to no longer have any qualities which could truly be called human.

Where Christians have intellectual difficulties with the idea of incarnation or with the union of two natures in one, the tendency is often to resolve them in the direction of Ebionism by exclusive stress on his humanity. This is also the case where an ethical interest is strong, because the humanity of Jesus as moral example is important. Where the chief interest is "redemptionist"—that is, is concerned with understanding Christ not so much as moral guide but as bringer of salvation—the stress is apt to be on his "true godhood." Since only God can save, one may be tempted toward a docetism which belittles or denies his true manhood.

Despite the apparent balance of the Chalcedonian creed, most orthodox Christology in western Christianity up to modern times has probably tended toward docetism. This is still the heresy which is most tempting to those in the more conservative fellowships. This can be demonstrated by the difficulty which those in these traditions have in dealing with the limitations which real humanity places on Jesus. For instance, many have difficulty with the suggestion that Jesus was less than omniscient, despite his own clear statements that his knowledge was limited. Also, the hesitancy of many to admit that Jesus had real human freedom (else he might have sinned and spoiled our redemption) or to think of Jesus as feeling the normal and necessary desires of the flesh points to a widespread docetic tendency. Those who have been influenced by more contemporary trends in thought, theological and otherwise, probably lean in the direction of Ebionism, adjusting the image of Christ to do full justice to his human nature, perhaps at the expense of any meaningful "god-ness."

CAN CHRISTOLOGY BE TRANSLATED?

The foregoing discussion has aimed at two goals. First, it has sought to make clear how and why the church found itself led to Chalcedon and what the religious meaning of

Chalcedon really is. Second, it has been intended, less directly, to confront the contemporary Christian and lay theologian with some of the verbal and conceptual difficulties in the classical formula. We have indicated that the two-natures doctrine has become increasingly difficult for contemporary Christians to make sense of. Now, this is true not only of the liberal but also of the most conservative Christian. The former may simply dismiss it as a relic from the past. The latter will probably cling to it confessionally but make no attempt to explain or understand it. The first response runs the danger of losing all historic connection with the faith of the past and of ceasing to be Christian in any real sense. The second invites the spiritual schizophrenia which has cut the nerve of so much personal faith in our day.

What is the task of the theological thinker (including the lay theologian) toward Christology? Is it possible for Chalcedon to be translated? If we have trouble with the traditional language of Christology, with the two-natures doctrine and with all its intellectual impediments, is it possible to express what Christ means to us and to the church *today*, and to do so in language which is both valid and fruitful? The answer is that if we have trouble with the traditional doctrine of Christ, then we *must* translate. As we have seen, nothing is so meaningless as a theology which has been handed down from the past unassimilated and unpossessed. We must never let ourselves become the slaves of an ancient formula. This is the point of anticreedalism. We *must* get beyond Chalcedon! It may well be that some of the language of the fourth century has lost its clarity and force. It may well be that we cannot use such terms as nature or divinity without creating confusion and conflict. Perhaps for our day a wholly different set of images will have to be created in order to say what Christ is to us and why we persist in being Christians. After all, the point is to communicate the Christian faith with clarity and force to ourselves and to our neighbors. Here is where the "you" in the threefold source-norm formula applies. What indeed is Christ to *you?* The answer demands that we come to grips with Christology anew.

But the greater the eagerness and the courage with which we undertake such a translation, the more careful we should be to recognize the limits which still apply. Not everything is Christian, and not all Christology is both valid and fruitful. In our attempt to say what Christ is for us, we must make every effort to be sure that we are not losing the religious heart of the confession. It is possible that our description of Christ may depart so far from the traditional confessions as to leave no common ground between them and us. If this happens, we must immediately suspect that either our theology is bad and needs to be redone, or our faith has passed beyond the limits of Christian faith. This is the point of creedalism. However we put it, the "you" in the formula must live in tension with the witness of church and Scripture.

Is there an irreducible substance which must be expressed in any really Christian doctrine of Christ? I suspect that there is, and to put it in the proper terms will reveal the inseparable relationship of the three major doctrines we have examined so far. The two-natures doctrine stripped to its essentials affirms that in Jesus the dilemma of human experience has been decisively answered. As true man, Christ reveals that God is concerned with human existence. As true God, he reveals that the power of evil and death have been broken. The uniting of God and man in the incarnation meant to the classical Christian the binding together of providential power and loving concern. And whatever shape our Christology may take, it can be neither Christian nor creative unless it comes to focus in the sovereign love of God, that is, unless it is able to assure us that God is involved in the currents of human life for our sake, and also able finally to direct those currents toward a meaningful fulfillment, with the preservation of all that is good and human.

CONTEMPORARY PROBLEMS
IN CHRISTOLOGY

The attempt to understand Christ and to express his meaning for our day has its own particular problems, and we can
conclude this chapter by a brief description of several of the
most pressing ones. The responsible Christian must work out
his own Christology in the light of these questions.

The Problem of God and the
Loss of the Transcendent

We have discussed in the previous chapter the difficulty
which many contemporary men have with the idea of transcendence. Yet so much of the traditional language of Christology, including that of the New Testament, suggests not just
a transcendent being who takes on flesh, but also a transcendent *realm*, an "up there" from which he comes to the
"down here." Jesus' own language—"I go to prepare a place
. . . I will come again"—seems to place us back in the
two- or three-story universe, as does the language of nativity
and ascension. John A. T. Robinson's popular little book
Honest to God has argued that this "up there—down
here" language is foreign to the thinking of modern people,
but just how really strange it is was brought home to me by
Bishop Stephen Neill. He has told of a stained-glass window
in a very old British church depicting the ascension of Christ.
At the bottom of the panel are the apostles looking up toward
heaven. At the top is a white cloud, and projecting from
the bottom of the cloud are *two bare feet*, all that presumably
remains of the ascending Lord. If the image has a touch of
the ludicrous to the reader is it not because there is no longer
any "up there" in our understanding to give meaning to this
primitive symbol of transcendence? How can the language
and meaning of transcendence which was expressed so

graphically by the older symbols of Christology be revital-
ized? Or can we find new christological symbols, more adequate to a new culture and a new cosmology, without losing
the heart of Christology?

Closely related to the loss of transcendence is the loss of
the sense of God. If God cannot be clearly conceived or experienced, what then is Christ? It is being suggested in our
day that Christology can be done without God, and it is
especially interesting that the men who have raised the most
serious doubts about the place of God in modern religious
thought have not found it necessary to wholly surrender
Jesus. Bonhoeffer, and after him van Buren, Hamilton and
Altizer, the so-called Death of God theologians, have continued to call themselves Christian and to build their own
religious commitments on some understanding of Jesus
without reference to God. Can one have Christ without God?
Scarcely, in any way reminiscent of traditional Christianity,
it would seem. But what can Christ be to a man who has lost
God?

The Problem of the Resurrection

As we have seen, the resurrection was the heart of the
preaching in the Book of Acts. While it by no means ex-
hausted the church's understanding of Jesus, it would be difficult to conceive the genesis of the church without the resurrection. We have also seen that the resurrection played a vital
role in the developing Christology of the early church.
Now, this concept has been an intellectual stumbling block
for some men in every age, but a number of factors, historical
and scientific, have combined to make such faith far more
difficult than before, and have left those of us who still persist
in a resurrection faith with the sometime feeling that we are
kidding ourselves. On both biological-physiological and historical grounds the difficulties are considerable. So deep are
the problems confronting modern men in regard to the

resurrection that a great many serious and wholly Christian theologians have frankly surrendered any literal understanding of it. Some have interpreted it as a symbolic description of the new quality of life through Christ in the here and now. We will have more to say about such a "realized eschatology" in chapter twelve. It is doubtful, however, that such a view says all that the original confession sought to say. Can Christian theology do without a resurrection? If not, how can it be made meaningful?

It is interesting that, after several generations of theologians who have been hesitant to wrestle with the scientific and historical difficulties of the resurrection, some of the younger post-critical theologians are taking a new look at the situation. Two leaders in German thought, Wolfhart Pannenberg and Jürgen Moltmann, spokesmen for the so-called theology of hope, have both argued that the resurrection is essential to a genuine Christian theology and that it is by no means inconceivable in the light of science and history, properly understood. They have contributed some valuable insights, especially in relation to the question whether a unique event like the resurrection—that is, one without parallel in human experience—can be believed by men who always judge possibility in the light of past experience. While it is certain, however, that scientific and historical dogmatism need to be reexamined and perhaps modified, Pannenberg and Moltmann have by no means answered all the difficulties which stand between modern man and the resurrection. Here is a question of major significance on which lay theologians of special expertise in the scientific or historical disciplines might well make a valuable contribution.

The Problem of the Uniqueness of Christ

As we have said, we live in an age of historical awareness. This means in part that we are aware of the roles we play, individually and collectively, in the weaving of the tapestry of human history. It means also that we are immersed in the historical process and aware that our understanding is subject to all the limitations that go with being historical. Such an awareness of limitation represents a remarkable change from the Middle Ages, when the Christian-European perspective was assumed to be the only possible true perspective. The success of Christian culture, coupled with a rather complete isolation of West from East, made it easy for our ancestors to assume that history was western history and that true value was Christian value. In such a situation it was also easy to assume that the sole axis of truth lay in the pivotal figure of that culture—namely, Jesus Christ. For the Middle Ages there were only two historical categories: Christian and heathen, or truth and error.

The gradually deepening encounter of western culture with other cultures since the sixteenth and seventeenth centuries has changed this outlook and led to a more modern view of history. It became apparent that there was a greater diversity and richness of cultures than had been imagined and that not all nonwestern and non-Christian culture could be dismissed as primitive or denounced as evil. Not only was a new appreciation for other traditions kindled, but a healthy humility was awakened in the West. One could say that we became aware that we were not *the* culture, but one culture among many, that we viewed history from a peculiarly western prejudice, and that there was no inherent priority to our perspective. A logical consequence of this discovery was the principle of pluralism in history. According to this axiom, every point of view is relative to its situation and none can claim to rise above historical relativism so as to demand exclusive authority. Furthermore, since every event in history is qualified by every other event, all events in principle stand on the same level. *No single event* has universal significance for the modern historian.

Now it is important to remember that we are *all* modern historical men, and these principles of historical humility

more or less characterize all our thinking. Thus the problems
which modern pluralistic relativism create for faith in Christ
are felt by all of us, whether they are clearly formulated or
not. Any claim of finality or absolute authority violates this
historical sense. I suspect that the timidity which charac-
terizes so much individual Christianity today reflects the
sneaking suspicion that we cannot ourselves make sense of
an absolute Christ in a relativistic age.

I deal with young Christians continually who are bothered
by the problem of the uniqueness and absoluteness of Christ.
How can he be the unique source of truth when all events are
finally on the same historical level? They can understand that
he could be unique in a special sense for *us*, since he is the
one who created the church and the one who founded our
particular faith. Thus like a great teacher who opened our
eyes to the truth, he can never lose his place in our own
hearts. But could *one* single event in a limited history be
truth for all men, especially since the only truth we accept as
beyond doubt today, namely scientific truth, is characterized
by its universality? Can particular historical events be more
than local illustrations of absolute truth? Can truth for
all men come from a Semitic tribe in Syria? Yet the church
is committed, as we have seen, to Jesus Christ as the key to
history, truth and salvation.

The problem is not merely academic. The moral dilemma
posed by the problem of the "heathen" disturbs many believers today. If Christ is the *only* way to God, then how can
it be just of God to have left the vast majority of men without a witness? One reason for the present crisis in missions
is the tacit belief of many Christians that though Christ is
the answer for us, surely their religion is the answer for them.
But how can such an outlook be squared with the church's
confession that no man comes to the Father except by him?
Thus one of the tasks of the Christian today is to find
ways of understanding the uniqueness of Christ which do justice to the traditional conviction that he is the heart of faith

and revelation, and yet take seriously the moral and historical sensitivity of men.

SUGGESTIONS FOR THOUGHT
AND DISCUSSION

1. Write out a statement of your beliefs about Christ. Then compare it with the Apostles' Creed or your church confession. What have you omitted? Was there a reason for your omission? What have you added?

2. How do you think of Christ? What "image" of him is most appealing to you, for example, the infant Jesus, the teacher, the healer and miracle worker, the crucified, the risen Christ, the judge? Why your preference? Does this preference say anything about your understanding of how Christ benefits the believer?

3. How serious do you feel the problem of Christ's uniqueness, discussed on pp. 198–200 is for Christians today? Is it a barrier to unbelievers?

4. Many modern men are attracted to Jesus but have difficulty understanding him in traditional christological terms. Some rather strange interpretations of him have appeared in recent literature and art. What should the attitude of the Christian be to such attempts to reinterpret Christ? Should any interest in him be welcomed?

Suggestions for Application

Arrange a showing of the brief film entitled "The Parable" prepared for the New York World's Fair by the National Council of Churches (available from most religious film distributors). Discuss as a group. Read, also, *The Feast of Fools* by Harvey Cox (New York: Harper Colophon Books, Harper & Row) especially chapter ten on "Christ the Harlequin."

Are these meaningful interpretations of Christ? Are they Christian?

Listen to the recent "rock opera" entitled *Jesus Christ—Superstar* (Decca Records, DX 7206). What is your reaction to the picture of Jesus presented? Is it a religious picture? Is it "Christian"? Should such works be welcomed or not?

CHAPTER ELEVEN

Understanding the Church
(Ecclesiology)

To be a Christian is to be involved with the church. Personal faith is usually born in a community of faith, and it has usually been assumed that discipleship carries the implication of membership in the institutional and social expression of Christian belief. Until the nineteenth century the necessity of the church was rarely questioned by those who accepted the validity of religious faith at all. This was true even when they were highly critical of the particular forms which it took in their society or when it fell under the control of corrupt and unwholesome leaders. The reformers sought not to destroy the church but to purify and reconstitute it. Even the more radical sects, which broke with both Roman and Reform churches, did not reject the church in principle. Rather, they sought to reestablish what they called the *Rechte Kirche,* "the true church," which they felt had been abolished by the powerful and replaced by a corrupt man-made institution. So although there was no common agreement concerning the church's nature, there was consent that it was a necessary and desirable concomitant of Christianity.

Such a consensus no longer exists. The concept of the church as a necessary expression of faith has come under challenge today along with the other central issues of faith, and a great many people who still have a strong commitment to the principles of Christianity or to Christ as Lord no longer feel much commitment to the church or involvement in it. Now, I am speaking not just of the practical noninvolvement of the marginal church member and believer, but of a conscious attempt to be Christian without the church. Some even feel that the only way one can truly be Christian is to repudiate the church as an institution. While most serious Christians have avoided such a repudiation, we nevertheless all feel to some extent the identity crisis which the church is presently experiencing. What precisely is the church? Is it a divine institution, redemptive and sacramental, through which alone the grace of God is received? Is it a purely human fellowship existing for the edification and mutual support of its members? What is the relation between form and function? Is its primary task evangelism or social amelioration? Or if both, how are these two tasks related to each other? Is the church necessarily *one* church, characterized by a unity received from its one Lord? Then how is its pluralism to be understood? All of these questions, arising with new urgency in the context of the present ferment, make this an exciting time for the lay theologian.

THE REALITY OF THE CHURCH

The branch of theology concerned with the church is called, appropriately, *ecclesiology* (from the Greek *ecclesia*, or church). Like the other central doctrines of faith, it was existential in its origin—that is, it was called into being by an accomplished fact of faith. Just as Christology was the church's response to the reality of redemption in Jesus, so ecclesiology was the church's response to its own reality, to the fact of its existence. Now, it recognized that it owed its existence to Christ, both in the sense that it could trace its origin back to the band of disciples which he had gathered, and in the sense that his redemptive work had paved the way for its existence. But it continued in existence after his ascension with his commission to evangelize and to live in anticipation of his return.

Even as the Apostolic church had no Christology at the beginning, it also had no ecclesiology. Here again, the early Christians had to move from the fact of the worshiping community to a doctrine which did justice to it. In one respect, however, the situation regarding a doctrine of the church was more complex than in the case of Christology. In a sense, the data relating to Christ had a kind of factual permanence. Who Jesus was, what he said, and what he had done were largely a matter of record. The interpretations of his person and work might change but they would rest upon a body of history essentially complete. Even the traditions concerning him became relatively fixed at a fairly early date. In the case of the church, however, almost nothing was fixed, and during the first few centuries, when its members were trying for the first time to understand what it meant to *be* the church, it was in a constant state of change. At the beginning it had little or no organization and few guidelines except the increasingly inadequate patterns borrowed from Judaism. It is little wonder that ecclesiology remained rather amorphous until the political and social situation of the church began to stabilize after about A.D. 300.

Nevertheless, there were certain aspects of the church's experience which remained fairly central in all that they tried to say about themselves and their fellowship. Above all, they understood that the community of faith was created by God. The church was no mere accident of circumstance, nor was it the result of human activity. It was a divine reality. Behind its origin lay the divine initiative without which it could have never been. Even as the Israel of old,

God's first covenant people, had been called into being by his mighty acts through Moses, the church, the new covenant people, had been called into existence by the act of God in Christ.

This divine initiative was expressed in two ways. First, the church saw itself as the continuation of Christ's work and therefore as being of divine origin. Furthermore, it understood its vitality and authority to be given to it in the person of the Holy Spirit. Since it was a divine creation and not a human invention, participation in its membership was also the result of divine initiative. Only the leadership of the Spirit could bring a person into its fellowship, and only the sanctifying work of the Spirit through its worship life could keep him worthy of remaining.

From this conviction that the church was a divine creation flowed the sense of mission which characterized its early years and the confidence which enabled it to survive and grow against great odds. But at the same time, the church was aware of itself as a human fellowship. This was true in the sense that it was a communion of believers, and that its members were bound together by a peculiar kind of closeness growing out of their shared sense of forgiveness and sonship. They called this special bond *koinonia*, or "fellowship-in-love." They were also aware that in a less affirmative sense they were a human fellowship. That is, though they called themselves saints, their fellowship fell short of the ideal character that it should have had as the people of God. Whatever it was in theory, it was in fact a struggling human society, filled with immature believers, torn by anxieties and frictions, and subject to all the ambiguities of the human situation. What was the relationship between its divine nature and its all-too-human character? Like all human fellowships it quickly developed structural and organizational characteristics. Leaders began to emerge and rules for its regulation appeared. What again was the relationship between this formal structure and the living fellowship which it regulated? The perennial problem of form versus content, of the church as institution versus the church as community of faith, of "visible and invisible" church began to take shape.

As the church became aware of its existence as a new creation of God it began to struggle to achieve a sense of its own character and identity. There is evidence of such a struggle in the New Testament. No definition of "church" as such is to be found there, but the church's growing self-understanding is reflected in a series of graphic symbols or analogies. Most of the analogies chosen have roots in Judaism, and reflect the degree to which the early church interpreted its mission in the light of the covenant faith of Israel. Most clearly indicating this sense of continuity with the people of the Old Covenant were a group of symbols which were basically enlargements of figures common to the Old Testament. For example, Israel had been the people of God who through ignorance or stubbornness of will had lost their redemptive role. The church was understood to be the new people of God, upon whom the mantle of mission had now fallen. As Israel had been God's flock, so the church had become the new flock and Christ her shepherd. The church is also spoken of as the household of faith and as the family of God, in which the believers are not only brothers but have been made God's heirs through Christ.

Each of these images in its own way comments on the character of the church both as a divine institution (a people is *called*, a flock is dependent on its shepherd, and a family is begotten) and as a human fellowship. Also of Hebrew origin is the graphic figure of the vine and its branches which Jesus borrowed, in all probability, from the walls of the temple court itself, where it was an inscribed symbol of Israel. But one New Testament symbol, more than any other, has tended to become central in the ecclesiological thought of Christendom. This has been especially the case in the Roman church, where it has influenced not only

ecclesiology but also the understanding of redemption. Its
influence on the non-Catholic fellowships, while less direct,
has also been considerable. I am referring to the symbol,
drawn mainly from the writings of Paul, in which the church
is understood as the body of Christ. ("And gave him to be
the head over all things to the church, which is his body"
Eph. 1:22–23.) The central place which it held in the ecclesiological thinking of Paul, along with the relative richness of
the symbol, has tended to give it a creative power which the
other symbols appear to have lacked. It is useful to us in
summarizing what the early church sought to say about
itself as the creation of redemption. What does this vivid
symbol imply about the church?

The Headship of Christ

Whatever the nature of the church, it looks for its power
and direction to Christ. The early confession that "Jesus is
Lord" affirmed that the church found its reason for being in
the headship of Jesus. As the body is regulated and con-
trolled by the head, so the church is not free to determine
its own purposes or to set its own goals. It is a divine
institution with a divine purpose and program. It exists to
serve *his* purposes and not its own. Thus the church as
Christ's body becomes a "continuing incarnation." In common experience the body is the means by which the self or
mind actualizes its intentions and relates itself to the world.
If a body becomes paralyzed—that is, is no longer under
the control of or responsive to the needs of the self—the
person becomes helpless and incapable of self-expression or
even self-preservation. As the body of Christ, the church is
to be the functioning organ of the head, and therefore the
means of the divine activity in the world since the ascension
of the risen Lord.

As the body of Christ, the church's primary task then
is to give expression to the deepest intentions of Christ

toward men—to be his body at work in the world. There-fore, the church's mission is the threefold mission of its Lord, namely, (1) to reveal the Father to men, (2) to be the redeeming and saving fellowship which mediates the forgiveness of God and the hope of life everlasting, and (3) to provide the abiding context of fellowship with the Father. It was through the incarnation of Christ that God was brought down to men. It is through the continuing incarnation that his presence is made available to all men.

The Dependence of the Body on the Head

Christ is not only the source of the church's mission, he is the source of its very being. Each person who by the Spirit of God comes into his fellowship becomes a "member." We use the word member to describe a person affiliated with a church, but we should remember its biological origin. The branch torn away from the vine withers and dies, and the member of the body which is "dismembered," or cut off from the source of life which is the unity of the self (the head) cannot live. So also the church, and each of its "members" receives life from him who vivifies the whole body.

The Unity of the Members

We have said that the early church saw itself as both a divine institution and a human fellowship. The former is clearly expressed in the image of the body of Christ, but the bond of fellowship one with another is also implied. It was their common participation in Christ as members of his body which was the basis of their unity one with another. Their sharing of forgiveness and grace made possible an overlooking of differences otherwise incompatible. Indeed, within the unity of faith the very differences con-

tributed to the growing richness of the fellowship, since in
a body every different member contributes to the wholeness
in his own unique but necessary way. Thus the understanding of the church as the body of Christ points to a unity in
difference under the lordship of Christ which reminds us of
that unity in difference which is the mark of the living God
himself.

THE MARKS OF THE CHURCH

If the above description of the church is an ideal one, it
is evident that this ideal of unity under God, of a holy fellowship following Christ's lordship and doing his will in the
world, was rarely a fact. The early church, or at least local
expressions of it, fell far short of the ideal. Paul had to
rebuke the Corinthians for their disunity and self-will. James
accused believers of perpetuating class distinctions which
belied the oneness of their Lord. More than one church
showed by its actions that its deepest desires and ambitions
were for its own well-being and comfort. Were these all-
too-human bodies really churches? The question began to
arise, "What constitutes a true church?" Can there be
counterfeit churches? If so, how can you distinguish the
false from the true? In what way does a false church imperil
the work of redemption and threaten the body of Christ?
Are all churches in some degree counterfeit? How can the
church detect its own shortcoming so as to call itself to
order?

One answer to these questions was to consider whether
there were reliable marks of identity which distinguished the
true church from the "ersatz" church. In general, there came
to be recognized as valid four fundamental marks which,
although variously interpreted, have been accepted by most
Christian fellowships. How do you recognize the true church
in the midst of the confusion of voices, each crying, "Lo,

here!"? The true church, it was decided, must be *one, holy, catholic* and *apostolic*. If the church is the divine institution arising out of the one decisive event of revelation, valid for all men and ages, then it must in some sense be, or *strive to be*, all of these.

Any attempt to define the church or to ask about its role in the contemporary world, must, of course, be prepared to go beyond this traditional formula, just as it cannot allow itself to be circumscribed too tightly by ancient formulas and creeds in other areas of theology. It may well be that ecclesiology needs new formulas today, or that the traditional formulas may be so loaded with misunderstanding as to be of little practical value. But once again, we must try to capture the essence of the traditional expression before we decide whether it is useful for theology today.

The Church as One

The unity of the church is the natural corollary of the headship of Christ. "For just as . . . all the members of the body . . . are one body, so it is with Christ." It is clear that of the many fears confronting the Apostolic church, few were as acute as the fear of schism. "Is Christ divided?" asked Paul. If there is indeed one Lord, and one Christ, must there not also be one baptism? Indeed, many of the most decisive developments in church order arose out of the fear of division within the ranks of Christendom. For example, the development of an episcopal structure, the formulation of creeds, and the fixing of the canon of Scripture were all maneuvers against disunity. For had not the Lord prayed to the Father concerning his disciples, ". . . that they may be one, even as we are one"?

How then are we to justify or even explain the divided character of the church throughout history, especially since it is a creation of the Holy Spirit? What should be the attitude of the believer today concerning a divided church?

Does its divided character and differences of outlook and belief discredit it and justify its rejection, or do they reflect simply an escapable human imperfection?

It is important, of course, to distinguish between kinds of unity. The classical church often failed to make a distinction between doctrinal unity and structural unity, partly because it recognized that differences in polity could reflect and even create differences in doctrine. The result of this confusion, however, tended to be the creation of an external, structural unity which was sometimes a little oblivious to human freedom and to its own changing content. It has been said, with some justification, that the Roman church achieved structural unity through the principle of apostolic succession, but allowed its doctrine to undergo substantive changes almost every generation. But if Romanism tended to deify structural unity, the Reformed and sectarian churches, partly in reaction, found their principle in unity of faith or doctrine. Coupled with the principle of individual competency, the frequent result of this was very little unity at all, since essential agreement could rarely be achieved except within the very smallest units of fellowship. Many modern Catholics, from the perspective of a church in which the structure of authority seems to suppress free expression and difference of opinion, look longingly at the free churches, while those in the free-church tradition, tiring of the babble of disunity which has become its hallmark for four centuries, sometimes find themselves longing for the structure of authority.

What ought to be the attitude of the church and the believer today toward church unity? This question has been a major one in twentieth century theology, finding expression in serious Catholic and non-Catholic confrontation. It has also found expression in the so-called ecumenical movement which has engaged both theologian and layman, and has produced some significant, if highly controversial, consequences. From these discussions has emerged at least one basic point of agreement, namely, that disunity must not be regarded as normal or good. It must be seen as a judgment on the church, and a reminder that it is not yet fully the body of Christ. Disunity has come to be seen by a growing number of Christians and church fellowships as a flaw to be overcome by the power of God. There is less agreement as to the kind of unity which should be sought and as to the structural and practical results to be desired. Some see the ultimate goal to be the abolishing of all sectarian distinctions between Christians and the reappearance of the unified church of apostolic days. Probably a larger number today are concerned with the achievement of a common spirit of respect and love rather than any structural oneness. Such a spirit would value and respect those elements in each tradition which give it its identity and which add richness and depth to the Christian fellowship. At the same time it would seek to find common ground, especially through worship and mutual cooperation, in the furthering of the gospel.

The Church as Holy

Since the church was a divine creation, empowered by the Holy Spirit, and made up of people who had been forgiven and sanctified (called saints, "holy ones"), the church was called God's *holy* church. The New Testament repeatedly urges holiness as a distinguishing mark of God's people, and the church of the first two centuries had a deep sense of being such a holy community. This sense was strengthened by their awareness of separation from the hostile world which surrounded them. Gradually, however, the church began to win its way into society and to baptize increasing numbers of those whose attitudes had been shaped by that world. With the growing influx of often half-converted pagans came habits and customs which had previously been looked upon as inconsistent with the Christian confession. The church was forced to come to grips with the problem of sin. If the

church is the *holy* church, can it accept or tolerate sin? And
what of a man once forgiven and declared a saint who falls
again into sin? Can he be forgiven again? At first efforts were
made to distinguish between *trivial* (venial) sins, which did
not discredit the church or require the expulsion of the
sinner, and *mortal* sins, those serious ones which could not
be tolerated. By the exclusion of mortal sin, the church
sought to remain holy. Finally it began to realize that sin in
its midst was both endemic and inescapable. How then
could it be the holy church and the redemptive community?

This question continues to confront the Christian today,
and is the source of much of the modern disillusionment
with the church. It is still by reputation and often by designa-
tion the holy church, yet the lives of its people seldom are
distinguishable from those of their neighbors. Furthermore,
as an institution its aims, policies, and actions bear all the
earmarks of other more worldly social institutions. Can the
church be so clearly of the world and still be taken seriously
in its claim to holiness?

What can the holiness of the church mean today, if it
means anything at all? One traditional answer has been to
deny that the church's holiness is dependent on the sinlessness of its people or their separation from the world. Indeed,
it is said, if the church is the continuing incarnation, then
such a definition of holiness is meaningless. Christ's own
holiness was achieved in the midst of life, among publicans
and sinners. Rather, it may be said, the church's holiness
lies in the presence, in the midst of this worldly and sinful
society, of an objective holiness, of an unequivocal and un-
ambiguous power of God. It is the presence, action or power
of God which makes it holy. If there is such an objective
holiness, which sanctifies and forgives us even while we are
sinners, then we are still the holy church.

What might be the character of such a holiness within a
church of sinners? Several answers have been given in the

past. In the Roman tradition, it has usually been the presence of the Holy Sacraments. Here by Christ's institution, it was held, was concentrated the transforming power of grace to make us holy. As long as the sacraments communicate grace the church is holy. In the Reform tradition the answer has usually been in terms of Holy Scripture. It is in the Word of God in Scripture that the "holy" resides, and a sinful church, if it has the Holy Scriptures, is still the church. In the free-church or Anabaptist tradition, the answer was sometimes more directly in terms of God's spiritual presence. The church is a fellowship of sinners who experience and have fellowship with God through the Holy Spirit, and this is the meaning of its holiness.

What can it mean today to speak of the holiness of the church? How does it relate to the task of witness and of involvement in the world? Does the church pursue its holiness today by withdrawal from the corruption of culture, or can the call to holiness be the call to follow Christ into the world? Does holiness in the final analysis point to the fact that the life of the church flows from the reality of the presence of God in the midst of the world? These are some of the questions with which a modern ecclesiology must deal.

The Church as Catholic

The catholicity of the church is closely related to its unity. Catholic means, of course, universal, and the universality of the church is rooted in the uniqueness of Christ as the focal point of God's redemptive work. Hebrew monotheism led finally to a universalism, since if there is but one God he must be everybody's God. So also if there is but one Christ, then there can be but one gospel, and that a universal one. Those churches which have called themselves Catholic have, of course, never achieved anything like a geographic universality, even within global limits, but their tenacity in employing the term points to a concern that the universality of the church be kept in view. How should it be understood today? The real meaning of the universality of the church does not have to do with geographic extension, but with the validity and applicability of the gospel. To say that the church is universal is to say that the answers to the dilemma of life which it provides and the reality of God which it makes manifest are valid and true in every possible human situation. The church is no longer catholic when there appears in history a man, a nation, an era to which the gospel is no longer able to come as the Word of God, or when the church no longer feels the universality of its commission. How is the universality of faith to be understood in the cultural pluralism and historical relativism of our world? This question is related to the question of the uniqueness of Christ discussed in the previous chapter.

The Church as Apostolic

This final mark of the church affirms its sense of being rooted in the event of Christ and its affirmation that it must always be in continuity with the community created by the crucified and risen Lord. It reminds us that we cannot be Christian if we sever all ties to the apostolic period which saw the birth of the gospel. This sense of rootedness has been amazingly durable in Christendom. Every church has sought to justify its doctrine, polity and existence by appeal to the apostolic community, and the most radically new departures in faith have seen themselves as returns to apostolic Christianity. Even the radical theologians of our day seem concerned to affirm a kind of continuity with the first century, and to convince us that if they do not say what the church said, they mean what it really meant.

Insofar, then, as Christianity is Christian it intends to be apostolic. The question for our day is in what way or ways should the church seek to be faithful to the Apostolic church? There have been groups who sought to restore in detail the life and practices of the first century. This is no longer physically possible, and surely such restorationism or primitivism is no longer desirable. Yet many churches today seek to approximate restoration by singling out one or more New Testament customs or procedures of worship as evidence of their apostolic character. With some it is their style of hair, with others their procedure in baptism or their primitive style of worship. Such attempts are usually marked by inconsistency, since in most of their ideas and practices they remain deeply rooted in the modern world. What is worse, such a preoccupation with the details of apostolic practice may prevent us from asking the deeper questions about what it means to be apostolic. What really determines whether the spirit of a church is apostolic? What are the essentials of an apostolic theology, one which expresses the essence of the early church's faith, even if in language it departs from the first century? Once more, these are the questions which we must confront if we are to understand the church and give it a strong theological basis for its ministry today.

THE CONTINUING CRISIS

The questions which confront the church today are partly rooted in the persistent problems of being the church in the world which we have discussed above. They are made more intense by the particular crises and challenges of the present age. As we have seen, many of the central affirmations of Christian faith are undergoing scrutiny in the light of a changing world and of its new attitudes and values. The church, which structurally and ideologically seems so often to be tied to the past, is therefore suspect. Its history of obscurantism and of alliance with the established political and economic order have led many to doubt its capacity to change and to serve the interests of humanity at large instead of those of the dominant class. Therefore the church as an institution has been dismissed by a growing number who are still sympathetic with Christian faith in general. Declining attendance in most major Christian bodies during the last decade or so suggests that a growing number of people, even nominally Christian, find the church filling no real need in their lives. We can mention here only a few of the key questions which need prompt and courageous examination.

How Is the Church as an Organization Related to the Church as the Fellowship of Faith and the Body of Christ?

The Reformers distinguished the visible church, identifiable by its external order and structure, from the invisible church, known only to God. The former had for them a real and necessary place as the vehicle for the preached word in the world, but the latter was the church in essence. How essential is the traditional structure? Must there be a structure at all? Does life always create structure? Can one be Christian without the church? Can one repudiate the institution and still be true to the church?

What Is to Be the Church's Form in a Changing World?

The external form of the church was shaped both by the inner demands of its faith and by the cultural situation in which it found itself. If the church is to minister to the new cultural situation, it must be willing to modify its form accordingly. Yet every change runs the risk of distortion, or of losing values which may be expressed in traditional forms. If change is to be positive and creative, and yet if the new order is to serve the same gospel, then criticism and re-

construction must be regulated by intense and honest theological preparation.

It may be that the church of the future will be so radically
different as to scarcely be recognizable to those of us whose
roots are in the past. Some speak today of an end to the
organized church. Is this a possibility, or must there be some
structure to give form and to guide the church in the fulfilling
of its role? Could the church survive the death of the
"church"?

What Precisely Is to Be the Role of the Church in the Present and the Future?

Is it to function as a redemptive agency? Is its task then
primarily that of evangelism? Or is it chiefly for our day an
agency of social betterment, with a task of contributing to
a human social order in which compassion and love are
meaningful constituents? If the social role is a significant
one, how is it to make itself felt? Is the church to be
socially quietistic and to seek through the personal lives of
its people to bring about a humanizing of society, or is it
desirable and necessary that it become actively involved in
programs of social change which seem to promise the creation of human values?

Of course, in the past the church has functioned in both
the above roles, evangelism and social change, but with
varying degrees of emphasis and often with little understanding of the ways in which they relate to each other. What
priorities should be given to worship? What forms should it
take? How can the communal or fellowship aspects of church
life be enriched? How can the evangelistic concern of the
church express itself? What forms should our efforts assume
to be the love of God in the world? All of these are questions
which need to be looked at with a fresh perspective. But the
aspects of the church's life to which these questions point will

probably call for some expression in any future form which its
ecclesiology takes.

SUGGESTIONS FOR THOUGHT
AND DISCUSSION

1. Discuss the list of basic ecclesiological questions on
pp. 204, 218–20 in the light of your church's understanding
of itself and in the light of your experience as a modern
Christian.

2. What should be the attitude of the Christian who feels
that his church is falling short of the ideal? Is there more
than one appropriate response?

3. Try to imagine a society in which the church as an
institution, at least as presently known, no longer exists.
What forms might Christian life and witness take? What
problems would the disappearance of the institutional church
present? What advantages might result?

4. Does God ever manifest himself outside the church?
Can the Christian ever learn truth about God or his work
from people or movements outside the church? Is it possible
that there are "saved" people outside of traditional Christianity?

5. What should be the primary functions of the church
today? Evangelism? Social transformation? The stabilizing of
society? Works of mercy and social betterment? What do
your answers say about your understanding of man, God and
Christ?

6. How much unity or doctrinal agreement is necessary
for a church to be a church? Is doctrinal disagreement ever
a sound basis for refusing fellowship? On what grounds
would you refuse to accept a member or decline to cooperate
with another religious group?

7. Are most divisions between denominations and faiths
today primarily doctrinal? How do you feel about efforts at
church union? Analyze your reasons honestly.

CHAPTER TWELVE

Understanding the Christian Hope (Eschatology)

I BELIEVE IN . . . JESUS CHRIST . . . who the third day rose from the dead, who ascended into heaven . . . whence He comes to judge the living and the dead. . . . I believe in the resurrection of the flesh and in the life everlasting.

So reads the "Old Roman Symbol," the most ancient Christian confession known. This early expression of faith, dating from mid-second century bears out what the New Testament establishes, that the Apostolic church was incurably eschatological. The word eschatology is a difficult one. Not only is there a certain clumsiness in the way it rolls off of an English-speaking tongue, but it is also weighted with a burden of negative associations. It suggests to many a grotesque and unwholesome preoccupation with visions and with crystal ball gazing. There clings to it the fragrance of an other-worldliness unfashionable today. The term derives from the Greek *eschatos*, which means the last in a series of objects or events. Therefore eschatology is that division of Christian theology which concerns itself with "last things," with the expected consummation of individual

existence in death, resurrection and eternal life, and with
the consummation of history in general by the return of
Christ and the setting up of the Kingdom of God.

Now, even the most cursory reading of the New Testament will bear out the contention that the early church was
concerned with these matters, and that it looked for a
consummation of Christ's kingdom probably in a very short
time. But how significant was that concern? Was the church's
interest in such matters rooted in its faith or was it merely
an inheritance from the Pharisaic Judaism out of which it
had come? Since such concerns are not keenly felt by many
people today, it is easy for us to conclude that they were
peripheral to the apostolic gospel. The church's burning
interest in the second coming may strike us as a nonessential
and sometimes rather bizarre addendum to a religion of love
and social concern directed toward the here and the now.
We are perhaps relieved when Paul finds it necessary to
rebuke the excesses of the Thessalonian church over matters
of the "not yet," and to require that they function as men of
faith in the "already." But we mistake Paul's intention and
we misread the New Testament if we fail to sense the depth
of interest in last things. One of the most positive results
of modern biblical research has been the rediscovery of the
eschatological dimension of biblical faith. The New Testament, like the early church, is incurably committed to a
future hope. It is eschatological through and through.

Despite this fact, there is no clearly worked out scheme
of eschatology in the New Testament. Instead we find a rich
and sometimes confusing collage of imagery and symbols
which at times seem to defy systematic examination. This is
partly because many of the explicitly eschatological passages
in the New Testament are couched in the colorful but
obscure language borrowed from Jewish apocalypticism, the
language of mythical beasts and heavenly manifestations (for
example, the Book of Revelation). But this lack of systematic clarity is also present in Paul and John. The New Testa-

ment is rich in imagery of death, resurrection, and eternal life, of judgment and reconciliation, heaven and hell, parousia and consummation, but from this richness no clear and consistent doctrine emerges. Furthermore, the Christian teaching on "last things" has never received a clear and decisive formulation comparable to that achieved by the ecumenical councils with reference to the doctrine of God and of Christ. There has been no really "orthodox" eschatology in the same sense that there has been orthodox Christology.

Now why has this been so? Why has there been a certain vagueness in the church's expression of its hope? At least part of the answer lies in the intangible nature of its subject matter. In a sense no area of theology is completely free from the problem of vagueness. Its subject matter lacks the kind of concreteness which a scientifically oriented society finds reassuring. Theology deals with relationships between selves and other selves, and it talks about intangibles like redemption and God rather than about stones and stars. But at least the relationship of self to self can be directly experienced and one's awareness of redemption can have experiential vividness at times. Eschatology, on the other hand, is two steps further removed from concrete experience. This is so because, first, it deals with the future, and the future is always inaccessible to us. We can never speak with the same clarity and assurance of things to come as we do of things past and present. Second, eschatology speaks of a future which is radically different from *any* past or present which we have ever known. To speak of the future hope of the Christian is not like speaking of tomorrow. We cannot predict precisely what tomorrow will be like, but we can conceive it. It will be essentially like today—the same natural and historical laws will be in effect, the same limits and possibilities will apply. But the future of which faith speaks is a future which is radically different and radically new. It is *eternal* life, it is the Kingdom of God. In this future the

inevitable accompaniments of life here and now are somehow transcended, including mortality, sin, suffering and perhaps even temporality and finiteness. Our attempts to
conceive such an existence bog down in the mire of our
present limitations. How does one think of life without
time or human selfhood without suffering or sin?

Then Why Have Eschatology?

Since eschatology is concerned with the inaccessible future, it has often been regarded as the most questionable
and speculative of all Christian doctrines. Indeed Friedrich
Schleiermacher put eschatological dogmas in a distinct
category of their own. He called them "prophetic doctrines"
because they lacked both the confirmation of immediate
experience (Who alive can experience life after death?) and
the clarity of thought (Who can think both continued life
and consummation?). To these doctrines he denied the
full status of theology. And perhaps he is right! If eschatological doctrine lacks both clarity and immediate confirmation, why have it? Gordon Kaufman has asked, rhetorically,
"Would it not be wiser in such dubious matters to maintain
a discreet silence? Who knows, or possibly could know,
what comes after the termination of existence here on
earth?" Why not concern ourselves exclusively with the social
implications of the gospel and seek to transform life in the
present?

These questions are legitimate ones, and the Christian
should be reminded by them not to forget the limitations of
his knowledge. Since we speak of that which in many ways
eludes our grasp, we should be moved to a becoming humility. There is no area of Christian doctrine where a gracious
modesty and lack of dogmatism is more appropriate than
in eschatology. Modesty? Yes, but not silence!

While the Christian is aware that he must be careful
what he says about the future hope, he is not allowed to

say nothing at all. He must speak about the future under God. Christian faith is necessarily eschatological since it is committed to the sovereign love of God which overcomes the ambiguity and brokenness of existence. In its broadest sense, the Christian hope is an affirmation of the purposiveness and the goodness of human existence. As we have seen in previous chapters, the Christian doctrines of creation, of God, and of Christ all point to the redemption of human life. They all point to the "end" of human history, in the sense not so much of "conclusion" as of the "goal" or purpose toward which life moves. They affirm that the gospel is the answer to the ambiguity of our existence which stifles our creativity and strangles hope. Even as men of grace, we experience and witness daily the power of life to confound hope and to crush out human values. And it is not only the world's power to destroy life by death but its power to pervert the creative and to turn existence into a living hell which confirms this tragic ambiguity. Life seems so devoid of direction. "It moves," as a student said to me, "but where does it go?" If the final word concerning life is absurdity, how can the human values of love, creativity and joy be prevented from collapsing into nothing? The Christian concern for eschatology is the conviction that the decisive word of the gospel is the conquest of the absurdity and directionlessness of existence.

The Christian cannot be silent because in the final analysis everything else in theology finally boils down to this: that in God, the ambiguity of life is overcome. Genesis begins with an eschatological assertion: that all creation is good and therefore redeemable. The New Testament ends with the good news that the last enemy, death, has been put under his feet. Everything that Christian doctrine has to say about man, God and creation points to the fulfillment of human hope in God. It is no wonder, as Tillich has pointed out, that one could begin his theology with last things. All theology *is* eschatology!

THE NEW TESTAMENT EXPRESSION
OF HOPE

Despite the lack of a clear and consistent eschatological scheme, there are nevertheless certain expressions of future hope which were commonly held in the New Testament church and which form the backbone of the early church's eschatology. Without attempting to resolve the many difficult matters of interpretation connected with these eschatological symbols, we need to comment on them briefly.

Resurrection

The resurrection faith of the early church had two primary focal points, namely, the resurrection of Christ and the resurrection of all mankind at the end of the age. The former was the basis for the latter. It is obvious that the resurrection faith of the Apostolic church had its roots in the late Hebrew doctrine of the resurrection of the dead, but the real force behind the Christian doctrine of the final resurrection was the reality of the risen Christ. Over and over again—in the sermons in Acts, in the writings of Paul, and in the Apocalypse—the resurrection of Christ becomes the "earnest" or guarantee of our resurrection in the last day. The tragic character of life which ends in death was seen to have been conquered because in him death itself had been overcome. In Adam all died, and thus mortality became the hovering curse of humanity; in Christ, all were made alive. Faith in the resurrection of Christ pointed to the conquest of death in the life of the believer. But it was clear to the Apostolic church, at least after the passing of a few years, that death was not yet conquered in its own ranks. Therefore, reinforced by Jesus' promises of the coming Kingdom of God, they looked forward to a time when death itself would cease to be and those who had fallen asleep would, like the Savior, be alive again to each other and to God.

It would be well to point out at this juncture of our exposition a fact which has become commonplace in theological discussion but which still sometimes comes as a surprise in lay circles. The primary New Testament way of affirming the survival of the person after death is not by a doctrine of immortality. Such a doctrine usually refers to the existence of an indestructible soul which resides in a body; but it does so in such a way as to not really be dependent on that body, so that it can continue a full and total existence apart from the flesh. Such an idea is rooted in Greek rather than Hebraic thought. Hebrew psychology is unitary. Man is a union of body and soul, and no really meaningful existence apart from "some kind of bodily state" is imaginable to the Hebrew. Thus while the idea of existence in a disembodied state is suggested in the New Testament, it never sits quite comfortably with the rest of apostolic eschatology. In keeping with its Hebrew origins, New Testament eschatology speaks instead of *resurrection*. The doctrine of the resurrection of the body suggests that eternal life in Christ is no ghostly existence apart from the body but a real and total being, a unity of selfhood, assured by the same power that called us into being at the beginning, namely, the creative power of God.

Parousia

The Greek word *parousia* means "presence" and is used in the New Testament in the sense of the "arrival" or the "appearing" of Christ at the end of the age. The early church felt that in Christ not only had the finality of death been overcome, so that the believer might hope for redemption in heaven, but that in principle the ambiguity of history itself had been overcome. Christ was the answer to the aimlessness and sorrow of corporate human life. It was all too evident, however, that the banishment of sorrow and tragedy was far from complete. Even in the church one had only an "earnest of the inheritance," a foretaste of blessedness. Therefore they looked forward to a time when God would finally wipe away all tears and when the ambiguity of history would come to an end because history itself would be at an end. The Christian hope looked forward to an end of history, not just in the sense that the historical order would reach a conclusion (whether with a bang or a whimper), but also in the sense that it would reach its *goal*, would achieve finally the potential which had been implied when God saw that it was good. It would be consummation and the beginning of the Kingdom of God. Since no consummation was conceivable apart from him who had conquered death, the end of the age was anticipated as the "second coming" of the Redeemer-Savior in final victory.

Judgment

For the New Testament church, Christ was not only redeemer but also judge. Since the only finally redeeming word spoken by God was spoken in Christ, and since in him alone it was possible to become an heir of God's promise, one's eternal destiny rested in him. Yet, clearly, not all would respond to the word of grace in Christ. Could one reject the promise of redemption or remain indifferent to the antonement made manifest in the cross and still see the Kingdom of God? The church's answer was a negative one. A person's relation to Christ was "crucial" ("cross-ly"). Therefore, the church taught that when the Lord appeared, he would find it necessary to make a great division by which the final destinies of men would be determined. Redemption for the believing implied the necessary and frightful corollary of rejection for the faithless and the reprobate. The imagery of judgment is varied and often colorful, but the deepest note of anguish is that of a decisive and eternal separation from the fellowship of God and from love.

Blessedness in Heaven

For the early church the end of history ushered in the final stage of things. To the faithful this meant a personal consummation within a living fellowship. The imagery which describes the consummation is rich and various. It speaks of "eternal life," in which the frustrations of life and the fear of death are overcome. It speaks of a heavenly existence which in poetic description often echoes the imagery of the original paradise. It speaks of the "Kingdom of God," stressing thereby the sovereign Lordship of God and the promise of a future filled with blessedness and ever-richer fellowship with one another and with God.

THE CRISIS OF HOPE

The person who writes theology today often finds himself wondering whether anybody is listening. We discussed in chapter one the attitude of indifference to doctrine which is often encountered even in Christian circles. This feeling is intensified when one is writing on eschatology. We have said that in some respects all of the major aspects of Christian theology are encountering difficulties because of changing views of life and of the world. This is true of eschatology with special intensity. Many people who find the Christian message of sin, forgiveness and love meaningful will admit that they are able to make nothing of the imagery of the second coming, resurrection, heaven and hell. There are a number of reasons why traditional eschatology has had difficulty making its way in recent years, and the Christian who is seeking to develop a personal theology has to reckon with these difficulties. We can only suggest the primary problems which demand courageous and creative theological thinking.

A Lack of Interest in Any
Other World than This

One of the evidences of the secular mood of which we have spoken is widespread satisfaction with the present life and willingness to accept the limitations of mortality. Now, we may dismiss such a "this-worldly" attitude as sin, but it nevertheless cuts the nerve of interest in a life beyond. Indeed, there are significant numbers of Christians who feel that a faith which concerns itself with achieving a fruitful life here and now is quite enough. This situation has no doubt come about in large measure because of the relative richness of modern life. When life was of few years and full of trouble, so that little sense of personal accomplishment was possible for most men, the promise of life to come had power. This is not so much the case today. Indeed, with many this very richness may produce a sense of satiation and boredom which may militate against a longing for greater fulfillment. In any case, there are many who deny any desire for or interest in a future hope. Indeed, it is sometimes argued that such a desire is itself an evidence of neurosis, and that the truly healthy person accepts his humanity and lives joyfully in the world, rather than fleeing its responsibilities and evading its opportunities in pursuit of another world. And it must certainly be confessed that the kind of Christian faith which is most preoccupied with eschatological speculation is often almost completely devoid of interest in the ethical and social concerns of the present. Does the gospel have a right to call men away from the present to a preoccupation with the future? And in any case, what has the Christian hope to offer to the man who "isn't having any, thank you!"?

*Problems of Conceiving an End
of Time and Life after Death*

Modern man's problem is not merely that he has trouble being interested in these matters. This difficulty might be overcome by a turn for the worse in history. There have been secular times before. The palmy days of the Greek city-state, with its ordered society and condition of general well-being, saw a similar disinterest in the "hereafter," but the disintegration of Greek culture put an end to that. Generally speaking, in the past the longing for fulfillment beyond death returned with the collapse of earthly hopes and values. The puzzling fact of the present situation is that even with the decline of optimism which has marked the middle decades of this century and the growing fear even for the survival of the race itself, there has been no widespread return to future hope. The problem seems to be that even if we feel the need to believe in a future hope we have trouble *conceiving* such a hope. The Christian eschatological symbols seem bogged down in a world view which is no longer real for us. How does one think of the return of Christ "in the clouds of glory" in a Newtonian world? Let us look briefly at the primary points of difficulty which the contemporary Christian faces in making eschatology relevant.

It should be pointed out that not all of the difficulty which modern man has with eschatology is rooted in biblical thought. Much popular eschatology has its roots more deeply in Greek and pagan traditions than in the Hebrew-Christian tradition. For instance, as we have commented already, the idea of the immortality of the soul is scarcely a biblical idea, so that the person who finds the thought of disembodied existence difficult is not therefore disqualified as a theologian of hope. Nevertheless, the difficulties posed by genuinely Christian eschatology are enough.

1. *Cosmological problems.* Some of the most troublesome difficulties relate to changes in our understanding of

the universe. The early church cast its message of hope in the "cosmology" of its day, that is, in terms of its understanding of the universe. First-century men viewed the cosmos as a three-story affair, with heaven a spatially definite place above and hell or the underworld below. In such a view it was easy to understand the nativity and ascension of Christ, and the coming down and going up of angels and souls. Nor was it difficult in such a universe to conceive the continuation of earthly life in another place, probably "up there" somewhere. It was also relatively easy for such men to think of an end of time and therefore a consummation of history, since their historical vision was at best rather limited. But the world in which we live is one that is virtually infinite in regard to both time and space. As radio astronomy pushes the limits of space beyond imagination it reveals that what lies beyond our most recent limits is a part of *this* universe, and is governed by the same conditions which govern our lives. The infinitude and unity of our world cause the sensitive person to wonder where in reality as we know it is room for the realm of eternal life. Where in heaven can heaven be? (And perhaps, thanks to the progress of modern earth sciences, do we now dare ask, "Where in heaven is hell?") Although this way of putting the matter may sound a bit crude, yet all of us feel the stifling effect of the "blanket of nature." If this one world is all that makes sense to us, how can we conceive another?

The same problem confronts us with respect to time. For the first-century Christian the time elapsed since the beginning of the world was very brief—in Hebrew terms only about two thousand years. It was reasonable therefore to conceive an end of time in the not-too-distant future. Thus the second coming and consummation could be both understood and anticipated. But what about men for whom the infinite geological and cosmic time of modern science is an accepted fact? Beginnings and ends cannot be separated. If one can no longer conceive a beginning, can he conceive an end? How can the language of eschatology be made meaningful in the universe of Newton and Einstein?

2. *Sociological and biological problems.* Most popular and many formal theologies have tended to understand man as a "spirit" or indestructible soul which is not finally dependent either on the body in which he "lives" or on the social situation in which he has come to be. Thus the death of the body and the loss of living social existence has not been seen as a serious deprivation. In past centuries there was relatively little difficulty in thinking of the survival of the self in conscious form without the body. This is not so easy any more. We have come to take more seriously the social origins of selfhood. We know, thanks to sociology and depth psychology, that our very identity is shaped by our social relations. I am nothing apart from the self I have *become* as son, brother, father, husband, teacher and friend. I have been created by my relations. How then can *I* survive if I am cut off from all these living relations which made me and which were mediated through the body? Furthermore, we have come to understand ever more clearly how dependent is consciousness and personality on body function. Man as we view him is not a soul living in a body but is somehow a "psychosomatic" unity in which bodily functions and personal consciousness are mutually dependent. We know today that physical and neural disturbances can alter personality and that consciousness and personal identity are conditioned by bodily states. If this is so—if all the subtle feelings and affections which we call self-consciousness are completely dependent on nerve cells and sinew—what can it mean to exist as a self after the body has returned to dust?

It has been a deep feeling for this problem which has led contemporary theologians to stress the biblical view of man as opposed to the Greek dualism so influential in much traditional eschatology. The Hebrew looked upon man as just such a psychosomatic unity. Properly understood, the doctrine of the resurrection seeks to affirm that there is

finally no selfhood, even after death, which is not a unity of
body and soul by the power of God. It is not clear, however, that this emphasis has had a very widespread effect in
making a future hope more easily thought.

3. *Moral and ethical problems.* Certain aspects of traditional eschatology have been seen by some to be morally
problematical. It has been objected that insofar as the hope
for eternal life is the selfish desire for reward and insofar as
it directs men's thoughts away from creative and responsible
living here, it is an expression of sin and not of grace. The
Christian must confess that the church has often harbored
an unbecoming "other-worldliness" and must agree that if
this is the only source of its hope, then there is an un-
wholesomeness about it.

Even more troubling for many today is the idea of judgment and eternal punishment. Few Christian confessions
have lacked entirely such a teaching. They have recognized
that somehow central to the gospel is the decisiveness of this
life, and have felt sure that the free commitments which we
make in our lifetimes have the power to shape the eternal
future both for men and for God. If the cruciality of Christ
is surrendered, what becomes of the whole structure of Christian faith? And yet a sensitive humanitarianism often finds
it very difficult to make sense of a punishment or a separation from God which is eternal. Can the sins we commit in
our finitude and ignorance have everlasting consequences?
An educative or temporal punishment could perhaps be
understood, as a parent might punish with a fuller reconciliation in view, but could an endless punishment be other than
vindictive? "Can we," it has been asked, "worship a God
who is less 'human' than we?" Nor is it merely the secular
humanist who has difficulty here. The problem is rooted in
the gospel itself, for it is Christianity which has taught us to
love all men, and to recognize that we all share equally in
the corporate guilt of sin. If in the past we were able to
make a sharp distinction between the worthy and the unworthy, between saint and heathen, this is no longer an easy

thing. The sense of human concern born in us through grace does not rest easy with eternal judgment. If in the final analysis the irreducible confession of faith is that "God is love," how can this be squared with eternal rejection of his creature?

4. *Theological and religious difficulties.* Some of the difficulties many feel in conceiving the Christian hope arise not so much from conflict with the modern world view or its mood as from seeming tension or conflict between elements within that hope itself. The chief example concerns what might be termed the central paradox of Christian eschatology, namely the tension between personal continuity and consummation. Christian eschatology has with great consistency affirmed two things. First, it has affirmed the continuity of the self after death. As a believer, I am assured that the self which survives death is the same as the self who died, that it is truly myself which lives beyond the grave. Second, it is confessed that the life which I know beyond death is a life of fulfillment and blessedness in which the ambiguity, fear and pain of earthly life is overcome. But these two ideas are not easily combined. How can I conceive of *this* self surviving apart from the social circumstances in which I came to be? And how can a life without temptation, doubt, fear, pain, risk, growth, and mortality be continuous with this life and with this self? Can I even conceive of life without these? The more we stress the continuity of the self the harder it is to understand consummation—or, it might be added, to desire it. A life devoid of growth or the excitement of the unknown might seem less like heaven than hell. To many people today the popular image of an eternity spent sitting on a cloud, strumming out perfect harmonies, is a picture of unbearable tedium. The more we stress blessedness and consummation, the less sense continuity with this life makes. How is it possible to do justice to both these affirmations, without producing a kind of mental weariness which is the threshold of disinterest?

REALIZED ESCHATOLOGY: IS ONE
WORLD ENOUGH?

In view of the difficulties confronting traditional eschatology, it is not surprising that the attempt has been made to modify or "translate" its central affirmations into language more congenial to contemporary people. One such attempt at reinterpretation is the approach sometimes referred to as "realized eschatology." As the term suggests, realized eschatology is an attempt to understand the Christian hope largely, or even wholly, in terms of a fullness of life here and now, rather than in terms of a life of consummation after death. Such an approach has much to recommend it. It offers the possibility of making eschatology meaningful to those who cannot conceive of or are disinterested in a life beyond. It avoids the accusation that Christians are unconcerned for the present life, by underlining the relevance of the gospel for this life. It can furthermore appeal to strong biblical elements. For example, it is now generally conceded by Old Testament scholars that Hebrew faith was without a clear concept of life after death until very late in its history. Also, there is an undeniable element of realized eschatology in the New Testament. This becomes especially clear in the most "mature" theological writing of the New Testament, the Gospel of John. "Eternal life" for the Fourth Gospel is clearly concerned with the quality and character of the life of the redeemed, and only in a secondary sense with questions of duration. It can also be said that many of the major theologians of the past century and a half, from Schleiermacher to Tillich, Bultmann and Hartshorne, have been tempted to go in this direction.

What can we say to realized eschatology? Is one world enough? At the very least we must accept it as a rebuke to an exclusive other-worldly hope and agree that unless the gospel can give men a sense of fulfillment and meaning for the present life it has no real message for that which may come. No one for whom this life is meaningless can hope for any meaning in another life. Fulfillment in the future is not finally meaningful apart from fulfillment in the present. We must as believers also affirm that to know Christ and to have fellowship with God through him is in a very real sense to partake of eternal life now. Furthermore, we must agree that the desire to escape the finality of death may arise from sin, and express a neurotic refusal to accept our mortality. If so, then it is the task of faith to expose such a subterfuge. But when this has been said not everything has been said. Despite the attractiveness of realized eschatology, it is doubtful that Christian theology can be content with such limited meaning. There are at least three reasons why it seems unlikely that the gospel can dispense with some form of future hope without seriously compromising its essential character.

The Deep Roots of the Future
Hope in Scripture and Tradition

It is clear that the church has *meant* to affirm more than a present hope. Realized eschatology is not all that there is in the New Testament. As we have seen, the eschatological hope—and largely futurist, at that—is the most fundamental note of the Apostolic church, as it has been an important expression of almost all Christian faith and thought until our time. Here is one instance in which the source-norm of personal experience comes under the scrutiny of Scripture and church.

The Demands of the Life of Grace

While the desire for continued existence *may* arise from sin, is not its deepest and truest source the life of grace? The nature of God revealed in redemption and the character of the relationship we have to God seem to demand some such faith. Is it not Christians, rather than non-Christians, who are most interested in the hereafter? Indeed, fellowship with Christ carries with it the conviction that God loves created selfhood, and that selves as the object of God's concern are of infinite value. The suspicion that God could suffer the obliteration of selfhood or that the relationship of blessedness which he has created could be less than eternal would endanger the image of the divine love.

The Incompleteness of Grace

The sad fact is that if consummation is a hope to be experienced *only* in this life, then it is an unfulfilled hope, and therefore a bitter deception. Fulfillment is never given to us here. Faith promises a life of authentic existence, one in which ambiguity and fear are overcome. We are assured by our faith that God will wipe away all tears from our eyes. This promise is never actualized on this side of death. A realized eschatology seems inadequate precisely for this reason: it is never realized. The Holy Spirit remains the "earnest of the inheritance" and not the inheritance itself. Thus that which we have (in hope) and yet have not seems to require fulfillment beyond the grave or else we must confess that it was after all a delusion. And what if the believer feels that the limited and fragmentary fulfillment of the life of grace is enough fulfillment for him? How can he be blessed in the awareness that the misery of humanity as a whole— a humanity which in grace we have come to love and to feel our kinship with—is to know no hope of respite or relief. If future eschatology without realized eschatology is meaningless, realized eschatology with no future hope seems a lie.

THE HEART OF THE CHRISTIAN HOPE

The problem of conceiving the Christian hope remains as one of the important challenges to the Christian thinker today, one that can benefit from the insights of lay theologians as well as the contribution of specialists in many areas of contemporary endeavor, such as biology, physics, psychology, parapsychology, and metaphysics. It may be that an adequate contemporary expression may take forms which will sound strange to traditional ears, but the efforts must be made, since the gospel says its decisive word when it speaks of its hope. In such a contemporary expression what is the irreducible core which a Christian hope must preserve? Any answer to such a question must necessarily be a personal one, but it is difficult for the writer to see how a theology could be called Christian which did not finally bear witness to the following themes.

The Seriousness of Life

However we shape our eschatology, we must do justice to the persistent note in Scripture and history that the gospel makes a difference, and that the work of Christ and faith in him are decisive events in the shaping of our destinies. How this element of seriousness is expressed (and whether *serious* must mean "ultimate") is perhaps open to further discussion, but Tillich is surely right that the symbols of judgment in the New Testament are not to be dismissed lightly.

The Permanent Value of the Self and the Persistence of Love

At the heart of Christian faith is the conviction that whatever the ultimate nature of reality, it is not indifferent to selves, and that selfhood finds a "home" in the universe. And this statement is none other than a philosophical translation of the ultimate confession of the Christian heart: namely, that God is love. If this confession is true, then no theology or eschatology is adequate which does not affirm the permanence of human selves and their persistence in the love of God. And such a confession is required not only by the sense of God's love for us but by the richness of fellowship one with another which we have come to know through him. Thus the experience of grace in the present points toward not only "eternal life" but an eternal fellowship in the Kingdom of God.

The Triumph of Life over Death

However the resurrection of Christ and the doctrine of the final resurrection are understood, it is clear that their central affirmation is that "death is swallowed up in victory." In a world where universal entropy or decay seem to be the rule, and where human affection and aspiration finally come to nothing in death, hope requires the assurance that life is the final word. But can't the victory of life refer to the indestructibility of the principle of life? Cannot the requirements of hope be fulfilled in the fact that though we men must die, *mankind* lives on? Does the victory of life mean necessarily the continued life of the individual? I think it does. In the past some comfort could be had in the face of death by the conviction that though we individually die, we live on through our contribution to humanity. But where is hope if, as so many signs today suggest, the race is mortal too? Somehow the final affirmation of Christian eschatology, and indeed of Christian theology is that "life is every Lord of death, and love can never lose its own."

SUGGESTIONS FOR THOUGHT
AND DISCUSSION

1. How did this chapter strike you? Did it seem of marginal importance? Were you less interested in it than, let us say, the chapter on man or God? Or was it more interesting? Why?

2. How important is a hope of life after death to most of the people you know, Christian and non-Christian? How important is such a hope to you? Could you be a satisfied Christian without it?

3. What would be for you a minimum eschatology? What do you feel the need to have affirmed about last things?

4. Is the distinction between immortality and resurrection (p. 227) new to you? Is it a helpful distinction or a troubling one? Ask yourself why.

5. Are there elements of traditional eschatology that you have trouble understanding or believing? Why? Is the problem scientific or religious?

6. Does the idea of judgment bother you? Can the love of God and eternal judgment be harmonized?

Suggested Readings

THE WORLD IS FULL OF READINGS which would enrich a person's faith and theology. I have resisted the temptation (mostly) to suggest readings in particular movements or men. This may come later. Most of the books listed below are general introductions to theology, its history, and to the major theologians of past and present. The listings are brief, rather arbitrary, and could be multiplied many fold. Most books below are up-to-date and many are available in paperback. Books likely to be especially useful are marked with an asterisk.

Theological glossaries or dictionaries of theological terms:

*A Handbook of Christian Theology. Cleveland: World Publishing Co., Meridian Books, 1952.

Harvey, Van A. A Handbook of Theological Terms. New York: Macmillan Co., 1964.

Richardson, Alan. A Theological Wordbook of the Bible. New York: Macmillan Paperbacks, 1967.

Systematic approaches to theology for the layman:

Barclay, William. The Apostles' Creed for Everyone. New York: Harper & Row, 1967.

Barth, Karl. The Faith of the Church. Cleveland: World Publishing Company, Meridian Books, 1958.

Brown, Robert McAfee. The Spirit of Protestantism. New York: Oxford University Press, 1965.

Brunner, Emil. Our Faith. New York: Charles Scribner's Sons, 1962.

*Forell, George. The Protestant Faith. Englewood Cliffs, N. J.: Prentice-Hall, 1960.

242

Hessert, Paul. *An Introduction to Christianity*. Englewood Cliffs, N. J.: Prentice-Hall, 1958.
*Kallas, James. *A Layman's Introduction to Christian Thought*. Richmond: John Knox Press, 1969.
Spurrier, William. *A Guide to the Christian Faith*. New York: Charles Scribner's Sons, 1952.
*Walhout, Donald. *Interpreting Religion*. Englewood Cliffs, N. J.: Prentice-Hall, 1963.
*Whale, J. S. *Christian Doctrine*. New York: Cambridge University Press, 1941.

Books on the contemporary theological situation:

*Barbour, Ian. *Issues in Science and Religion*. Englewood Cliffs, N. J.: Prentice-Hall, 1965.
————, ed. *Science and Religion*. New York: Harper Forum Series, 1968.
Birch, Charles L. *Nature and God*. Philadelphia: Westminster Press, 1965.
Jenkins, Daniel. *Beyond Religion*. Philadelphia: Westminster Press, 1962.
————. *The Christian Belief in God*. Philadelphia: Westminster Press, 1963.
————, ed. *The Scope of Theology*. Cleveland: World Publishing Co., 1965.
Jenkins, David. *Guide to the Debate about God*. Philadelphia: Westminster Press, 1966.
*Williams, Daniel D. *What Present Day Theologians Are Thinking*. 3rd ed., rev. New York: Harper Chapelbooks, 1967.

Introduction to today's leading theologians:

Hunt, G. L. *Ten Makers of Contemporary Theology*. New York: Association Press, 1958.
*Marty, Martin and Peerman, Dean, eds. *Handbook of Christian Theologians*. Cleveland: World Publishing Co., Meridian Press, 1967.

In addition to the survey-type books above, two excellent series of paperback books have recently appeared which seek to introduce the reader to important figures in twentieth-century religious thought. Each brief book deals with a single theologian or philosopher. A letter to the publisher will bring a complete listing. The series are:

Makers of Contemporary Theology published by John Knox Press, Richmond, Virginia. This series includes books on Paul Tillich, Martin Buber, Rudolf Bultmann, Dietrich Bonhoeffer, Pierre Teilhard de Chardin, and others.

The Promise of Theology published by J. B. Lippincott, Philadelphia, Pennsylvania. This series includes books on Karl Barth, John Bennett, Dietrich Bonhoeffer, Martin Buber, Rudolf Bultmann, Sören Kierkegaard, H. Richard Niebuhr, Reinhold Niebuhr, and Paul Tillich.

For those who want to sample the writings of some of these theologians, the following books of selections are suggested:

Eckart, Roy A., ed. *The Theologian at Work.* New York: Harper Forum Series, 1968.

Galloway, A. D., ed. *Basic Readings in Theology.* New York: Fernhill Press, 1964.

Some sources on the history of Christianity and Christian thought:

*Bainton, Roland. *Christendom,* 2 vols. New York: Harper Torchbooks, 1966.

Frend, W. H. C. *The Early Church.* Philadelphia: J. B. Lippincott, 1966.

*Lohse, Bernard. *A Short History of Christian Doctrine.* Philadelphia: Fortress Press, 1966.

McGiffert, A. C. *A History of Christian Thought.* 2 vols. New York: Charles Scribner's Sons, 1932.

*Welch, Claude and Dillenberger, John. *Protestant Christianity*. New York: Charles Scribner's Sons, 1954.

For brief readings from great theologians of other centuries the following is suggested:

Ferm, Robert. *Readings in the History of Christian Thought*. New York: Holt, Rinehart & Winston, 1964.

Glossary

THE WORD LIST below contains for the most part words which occur in this book without full explanation. As the reader progresses in his theological reading he may want to consult the fuller theological lexicons listed in the reading list on page 242. The definitions below are brief and avoid technical complexity whenever possible. Where a term has multiple meanings, the one given is that most pertinent to Christian theology.

Anthropomorphic. (Greek: "man-shaped") Language is said to be anthropomorphic when it attributes human characteristics to nonhuman beings. In reference to God, language is anthropomorphic when God's actions or his nature are described in human terms ("God's strong arm," "God repented himself"). Such language is often viewed as inadequate or unworthy of God, but it is likely that all language about God has some anthropomorphic element.

Apologetics. (Greek: "to speak for") The rational defense of theology or of Christianity from criticism or attack. As a kind of theology, apologetics is interested not only in proclaiming the gospel (see *kerygmatic theology*) but also with seeking to persuade men of its reasonable character and its truth.

Arianism. An early understanding of the Trinity or of Christology associated with Arius of Alexandria. Arius denied the full deity of the Logos (Christ), teaching that he was a created being who acted as God's agent in creation. The orthodox doctrine of the Trinity was hammered out at the Council of Nicaea (A.D. 325) in opposition to Arianism.

Barthianism. A type of theology associated with Karl Barth, late Swiss theologian. One of the dominant theological views of the present century, Barthianism stresses proclamation rather than apologetics, and is critical of most efforts to accommodate the gospel message to the values and outlooks of modern culture. (Also called Neo-Reformation theology, and crisis theology. See *kerygmatic theology.*)

Biblical criticism. A method of studying the Bible which seeks to apply the same rules of scholarly and historical analysis that are applied to nonbiblical historical documents. Biblical criticism takes seriously the human character and historical development of biblical writings, and seeks to answer questions which pertain to this human aspect, for example, dates and authorship, reliability of the texts, etc. Since critical studies have made clear the human dimension of biblical writings, they have called into question some theories of scriptural authority, such as scientific infallibility or verbal inerrancy. Post-critical theology accepts the validity of the biblical critical method.

Cosmology. (Greek: "world" or "universe") One's understanding or conception of the universe.

Determinism. A belief that all events in nature and history are the necessary results of prior causes. Since all things are predetermined, this view denies any real freedom or novelty in human life or in the universe.

Developmentalism. Any theory which looks upon the universe as dynamic and subject to development. Developmentalism usually maintains that the present state of things is the result of a lengthy development or evolution from prior states. Darwinism is one kind of developmental-ism.

Dialectical theology. See *Barthianism.*

Docetism. (Greek: "to seem") This word usually refers to a christological belief which denies or belittles the real humanity of Christ, usually on the ground that the flesh is evil and unworthy to receive the divine. (See *Dualism.*) Docetism therefore denies a real incarnation of God in Christ. God only *seemed* to become man.

Dualism. A word with many meanings. Philosophically it means a theory that there are two ultimate powers or realities which are equal in power or being and in eternal tension with each other. These powers may be given various designations, for example, darkness and light (Zoroaster), matter (or flesh) and spirit (Gnosticism), or God and Satan (some forms of biblicism). Biblical faith rejects dualism because it offers no final hope for the triumph of God and human meaning.

Ebionism. An early Christology, influenced by Jewish thought, which questioned the deity of Christ, preferring to understand him as the last and greatest of the prophets. The word has come to mean generally any opinion which belittles the divinity of Christ. (See *Docetism.*)

Economic Trinity. See *Functional Trinity.*

Empiricism. A theory of knowledge which teaches that all true knowledge is derived from sense experience and rejects as real any idea which cannot be tested and verified by sensory data. Most scientific thought is empirical. (See *Idealism.*)

Existential. An adjective derived from the philosophy known as Existentialism, which stresses actual lived experience rather than logic or theory as a source of truth. Thus existential has come to mean that which is personally experienced and in which one is deeply involved as a person. Involvement is felt to provide a truer understanding of reality than abstract observation.

Functional Trinity. A way of understanding the Trinity which looks upon the three "persons" in the godhead as three ways in which God relates to men or acts toward them, rather than as metaphysical distinctions in the divine. (Also called *Economic Trinity.*) Sometimes called *modalism,* such a view is not the same as *heretical modalism* (*Sabellianism*) since these "functions" are seen to be real and permanent aspects of God.

Gnosticism. A philosophy and religion of New Testament times which influenced early Christianity. It was usually dualistic, teaching that the soul is a prisoner of this worldly sphere, which is by nature evil. The soul can be delivered for return to the divine sphere by a secret *gnosis,* or wisdom. Christian Gnosticism tended to be docetic in Christology. Because of its negativism toward the world and its questionable Christology it was rejected by the main body of the church.

Humanism. A word of such various usages as to defy brief description. Two meanings which occur frequently in theological discussion are: (1) An attitude of respect for humanity and concern for the well-being of people, (2) a philosophical or religious conviction that man is the sole source of truth and value, that all truth must be affirmed by the human understanding unaided by revelation, and that human selfhood and society are of value in themselves, apart from reference to God.

Idealism. In philosophy or theology idealism refers to a theory of knowledge opposed to *empiricism.* It holds that the most trustworthy source of knowledge is the mind and its ways of thinking. Idealism feels that empirical data can only be trusted if it conforms to the order and structure of logic.

Immanence. The early church understood its hope to be dependent on two facts: that God was (1) sufficiently independent of the world to be free from its problems and able to direct its destiny, and (2) actively involved in that world in order to sustain, control, and redeem it. The independence of God is spoken of as his *transcendence*, his active presence as his *immanence*. Both ideas are necessary in any adequate Christian understanding of God.

Incarnation. (in-flesh) The Christian doctrine that in Jesus Christ God entered into or took on flesh for man's redemption.

Kerygma. (Greek: "proclamation") In contemporary theology *kerygma* has come to designate the essential proclamation of the church, especially as reflected in the New Testament. It included the declaration of the messiahship of Christ, the announcement of his resurrection, the promise of the Kingdom of God and a call to repentance and faith. The term *kerygmatic theology* is used today to describe theologies which stress proclamation or preaching, rather than apologetics. (See *Barthianism.*)

Liberalism. A broad variety of Christianity and theology which was most prevalent during the nineteenth and early twentieth centuries. It was characterized by a general confidence in man and in human reason, a willingness to revise traditional theology in the light of modern knowledge, and a general optimism about human society and its future. Its dominance was ended by World War I and by the attacks of neoorthodoxy.

Logos. A Greek term with a long history. It means "word, discourse or reason." In Stoic philosophy it designated the supreme rational principle or power at the heart of the universe. The New Testament writers, especially in the Gospel of John, applied the word to Jesus as the one who reveals the ultimate character of God. In subsequent centuries the term came to refer to the second person of the Trinity who became incarnate in Jesus.

Materialism. The teaching that all reality consists of matter or some expression or manifestation of matter. A true materialism views mind or spirit as a by-product of matter or as some expression of material activity.

Metaphysics. The branch of philosophy which tries to discover and describe the most universal and basic aspects of reality. Classic metaphysics seeks to ask what the nature of reality is so as to provide a solid foundation for the particular truths of life and nature. Since theology is also concerned with finding the ultimate foundations of human existence, it is doubtful that it can avoid metaphysical thought in some form.

Memento mori. "Remember death." The traditional stress of the church on the transitory character of life and the necessity of preparing the soul for eternity.

Modalism. See *Functional Trinity.*

Monism. The philosophical or religious teaching that all reality is ultimately one and that all particular things are manifestations of that one. Monism often denies the reality of particular things, seeing them as finally absorbed into the featureless unity of the absolute.

Monotheism. Belief in one God. In a true monotheism all created things come from God and are ultimately subject to his sovereign control.

Myth. A troublesome term since it means to most lay people a fantasy or falsehood. It has a much more positive meaning in theology. It points to the fact that no human language adequately speaks of God because it is limited to time and space. Thus, all religious language is the language of myth, being in some respects not literally true, and yet the necessary language for the expression of truths deeper than literal language can express.

Natural revelation. The revelation of God's existence, nature or purpose in the natural order (including human nature) in contrast to special revelation through Christ or through Scripture. Some theologians deny that God reveals himself through nature, or at least that such revelation can be comprehended without special revelation. Theology based on natural revelation is called natural theology.

Neoorthodoxy. A theological movement initiated about 1918 which rejected theological liberalism and sought to return to a theo-centric (God-centered) theology similar to that of the Reformation. (See *Barthianism, Neo-Reformation theology.*)

Neo-Reformation theology. See *Barthianism, Neoorthodoxy.*

Ontology. (Greek: "study of being") Metaphysics.

Orthodoxy. (Greek: "right teaching") In general, the opposite of heresy, especially teachings which conform to the official teachings of a church or denomination. It has sometimes come to mean the more conservative or traditional theology of a group or of the church.

Panentheism. A theory of God's relation to his world which seeks to avoid the problems of theism and pantheism. It sees all of creation as somehow within the divine life, yet sees God as still distinct from his world and in control.

Pantheism. (Greek: "everything is God") Classic pantheism believes that all things are modes of the divine, and that the divine in no way transcends nature. Thus God and nature are believed to be identical. Christian theology has generally rejected pantheism since it fails to distinguish God from his creation and denies personhood or distinct existence to God.

Paraclete. From the Gospel of John, the word means "one who accompanies," referring to the Holy Spirit as the companion and guide of the believer after the departure of Christ.

Paradox. (Greek: "against opinion") This term has many shades of meaning. Generally in philosophy or theology it refers to an opinion, concept or doctrine which appears to be logically contradictory but experientially undeniable, or one in which necessary elements of the idea are in tension with one another. In Christian faith the incarnation of the Divine in a finite person is often considered the essential paradox. Paradox may also refer to statements which are in different respects true and false: e.g., Jesus' statement, "He that saveth his life shall lose it, he that loseth it . . . shall find it."

Personalism. The belief or teaching that the ultimate reality at the heart of the universe is a person or at least is basically personal in nature. Most Christian theology is personalistic.

Post-critical. See *Biblical criticism.*

Rationalism. This term can mean: (1) any philosophy or attitude which values reason and holds it to be the ultimate criterion of truth, or (2) a philosophical view which holds that the ideas of the mind and the rules of thought and logic are a more reliable source of truth than the senses. (See *Idealism.*)

Reductionism. The tendency to escape the complexity of experience by denying the reality of one or more aspects of that experience, or by reducing one aspect to another. For example, a reductive materialism or naturalism might account for mind as nothing but atoms in action, or a reductive idealism might account for matter as nothing but the thoughts of God.

Theism. A theory which affirms that God is a distinct being, usually personal in character, who is creator and sustainer of the world. Most Christian theology is theistic.

Transcendence. See *Immanence.*